The Czechoslovak Cookbook

CROWN CLASSIC COOKBOOK SERIES

General Editor: CHARLOTTE ADAMS

The Czechoslovak Cookbook

by Joza Břízová, et al.

translated and adapted by
Adrienna Vahala

General Editor: Charlotte Adams

CROWN PUBLISHERS, INC., NEW YORK

CONTENTS

SOUPS AND
SOUP ACCOMPANIMENTS

BEEF SOUP (WHITE OR BROWN)
HOVĚZI POLÉVKA

6 cups cold water	½ medium celery root
1 pound beef (chuck or rump)	1 medium onion
	salt to taste
½ pound soup bones	1 tablespoon shortening
2 ounces liver	¼ cup rice, barley, farina,
2 carrots	or tapioca (for
1 parsnip	thickening)

For White Beef Soup, place meat, bones, and liver in water, cover, and bring slowly to a boil. Simmer for 2 or 3 hours. Strain; add salt. Dice meat and vegetables, and add to the broth; cook 8 to 10 minutes longer, or until vegetables are tender. Add chosen thickening agent, and cook until done.

For Brown Beef Soup, follow instructions for White Beef Soup, but fry the diced vegetables in the shortening before adding to broth. Add chosen thickening agent and cook until done. Serves 4 to 6.

CARAWAY SOUP
KMÍNOVÁ POLÉVKA

¼ cup butter	salt to taste
¼ cup flour	1 teaspoon caraway seeds
5 cups water or soup stock	1 cup cooked noodles

Brown butter in flour. Add water or stock, salt, and caraway seeds. Simmer for 20 to 30 minutes. Add noodles before serving. Serves 4 to 5.

1

CREAMED MEAT SOUP
MASITÁ POLÉVKA BÍLÁ

½ pound beef
6 cups water
2 cups diced vegetables
(carrot, parsnip,
celery root, cauli-
flower, peas, onion)
¼ cup butter

¼ cup flour
1 egg yolk
½ cup milk or cream
salt to taste
1 tablespoon minced
parsley

Simmer beef in salted water until tender (about 2 hours). Strain. Melt butter, blend in flour, and add to soup. Simmer for 20 minutes more. Add vegetables, and simmer for 10 minutes more. Beef can be diced and returned to soup, or served, sliced, to 2 persons, with a sauce or creamed vegetables as a main course. Before serving soup, add egg yolk, beaten with the milk or cream, and parsley. Do not boil again. Serves 4 to 6.

CREAMED SWEETBREADS SOUP
BRZLÍKOVÁ

Make like Creamed Meat Soup (above), but use ½ pound sweetbreads in place of the beef. Wash and skin sweetbreads; dice, and put into prepared soup. Serves 4 to 6.

CREAMED BRAINS SOUP
MOZĚCKOVÁ

Make like Creamed Meat Soup (above), but substitute ½ pound brains for the beef. Prepare the brains by pouring boiling water over them; drain and skin. Fry in 1 tablespoon butter with ½ chopped onion. Add to cooked soup. Serves 4 to 6.

CREAMED RAGOUT SOUP
Z TELECÍHO MASA

Make like Creamed Meat Soup (see Index), but use ½ pound veal in place of the beef, and simmer it for 45 minutes. Dice; add to prepared soup, and add a dash of mace. Serves 4 to 6.

CREAMED FISH SOUP
RYBÍ POLÉVKA

Make like Creamed Meat Soup (see Index), but use ½ pound fish in place of the meat. Simmer fish until tender (about 30 minutes). Add roe (if you have any) to soup when you add vegetables. Bone and dice fish; return to soup. Add a dash of mace. Serve with croutons. Serves 4 to 6.

FRIED FARINA SOUP
POLÉVKA Z PRAŽENÉ KRUPICE

1 cup chopped soup greens	salt to taste
¼ cup butter	1 teaspoon soy sauce
½ cup farina	1 tablespoon minced parsley
4 cups water	

Fry vegetables in butter. Add farina, and fry until golden. Add water and salt. Simmer for about 20 minutes. Before serving, add soy sauce and parsley. Serves 4 to 6.

GARLIC SOUP
ČESNEČKA

1 pound potatoes	4 cloves garlic
6 cups water	salt
dash of powdered cara-	4–6 slices toasted rye
way seeds	bread
¼ cup lard	

Dice potatoes. Boil in salted water with caraway seeds until tender (20 to 30 minutes). Add lard. Mash garlic with a pinch of salt and add to soup. Serve with toasted rye bread. Serves 4 to 6.

GIZZARD SOUP
POLÉVKA Z DRŮBEŽÍCH DRŮBKŮ

6 cups cold water	½ medium celery root,
gizzard, neck, wings,	cut up
and back of chicken,	1 medium onion, cut up
duck, turkey, or	¼ cup very thin noodles or
goose	rice
salt to taste	dash of mace
2 carrots, cut up	1 tablespoon minced
1 parsnip, cut up	parsley

Put well-cleaned gizzard, neck, wings, and back into water. Add salt and vegetables. Simmer for 2 to 3 hours or until tender. Strain soup, purée vegetables through strainer, remove meat from bones, dice. Return vegetables and meat to soup. Thicken soup by adding noodles or rice, and cooking until done. Add mace and parsley before serving. Serves 4.

GOULASH SOUP
GULÁŠOVÁ POLÉVKA

2 onions, chopped
2 tablespoons butter
¼ teaspoon paprika
1 pound diced beef
  (chuck or shank)
¼ cup butter
¼ cup flour
6 cups boiling water

1½ cups diced vegetables
  (carrot, parsnip,
  celery root)
salt to taste
1 pound diced potatoes
¼ teaspoon celery seed
dash of pepper

Fry onion in the 2 tablespoons butter. Add paprika and meat. Cook slowly until brown (about 30 minutes). Melt the ¼ cup butter, blend in flour, and fry until golden, stirring constantly. Add to meat with water, vegetables, and salt. Simmer for 20 minutes. Add potatoes, caraway seeds, and pepper, and simmer until potatoes are tender (20 to 30 minutes). Serves 4 to 6.

KIDNEY SOUP
LEDVINKOVÁ POLÉVKA

1 pound beef or pork
  kidneys
2 tablespoons butter
2 medium onions,
  chopped
¼ teaspoon caraway
  seeds
¼ teaspoon paprika

¼ cup butter
¼ cup flour
6 cups boiling water
1½ cups diced vegetables
  (carrot, parsnip,
  celery root)
salt to taste
croutons

Slice well-cleaned kidneys and brown with onion, caraway seeds, and paprika in the 2 tablespoons butter. Brown flour in the ¼ cup butter and add to kidneys with boiling water and vegetables. Simmer for 20 to 30 minutes. Before serving, add salt and croutons. Serves 4 to 6.

LEGUME SOUP
LUŠTĚNINOVÁ POLÉVKA

½ pound legumes (lentils,
    beans, or dried peas)
6 cups water
1 cup grated vegetables
    (carrot, onion,
    parsnip, celery root)

3 tablespoons flour
4 tablespoons butter
salt to taste
1 clove minced garlic
½ cup milk
croutons

Simmer legumes slowly in water until tender (1½ to 2 hours). Rub through strainer. Brown flour in butter, add to soup. Add vegetables. Simmer for 10 to 20 minutes. Stir in salt, garlic, and milk. Serve with croutons. Serves 4 to 6.

LIVER SOUP
JÁTROVÁ POLÉVKA

1 pound beef or pork
    liver
2 tablespoons butter
2 onions, chopped
¼ cup flour
¼ cup butter
6 cups boiling water

1½ cups diced vegetables
    (carrot, parsnip,
    celery root)
1 egg yolk
¼ teaspoon pepper
salt to taste

Cut liver into small strips. Brown well in the 2 tablespoons of butter with the onion. Brown flour in the ¼ cup butter. Add to liver with boiling water and vegetables. Simmer for 20 to 30 minutes. Before serving, add egg yolk, pepper, and salt. Serves 4 to 6.

MOCK BEEF SOUP
POLÉVKA Z KOSTÍ, NEPRAVÁ HOVĚZÍ

6 cups water
1 pound soup bones
   salt to taste
2 carrots, diced
1 parsnip, diced

½ medium celery root,
   diced
1 medium onion, diced
1 tablespoon shortening
¼ cup rice or barley
   (optional)

Put bones into cold water, bring slowly to a boil; simmer for 2 to 3 hours. Strain soup. Brown vegetables in the fat, add to soup. Add salt to taste. Thicken soup by adding rice or barley (or thicken with Liver Dumplings or Liver Rice [see Index]), and cook until done. Serves 4.

OXTAIL SOUP
POLÉVKA Z OHÁŇKY

6 cups water
1 pound oxtails
2 carrots, diced
1 parsnip, diced
½ medium celery root,
   diced
1 medium onion, diced

1 tablespoon shortening
3 peppercorns
1 small cauliflower or
   1 cup green peas
¼ pound mushrooms
1 tablespoon minced
   parsley

Cut oxtail into pieces and cook in water until tender (about 2 hours). Fry carrots, parsnip, and celery root in shortening with peppercorns. Strain soup. Remove meat from bones and cut into small pieces. Return meat and vegetables to soup, add cauliflower or peas and mushrooms; cook until tender (10 to 15 minutes). Add parsley. Serves 4.

QUICK BEEF SOUP WITH GROUND BEEF
RYCHLÁ HOVĚZÍ POLÉVKA
Z MLETÉHO MASA

6 cups cold water	1 medium onion, diced
½–¾ pound ground beef	1 tablespoon minced
2 carrots, diced	parsley
1 parsnip, diced	1 tablespoon shortening
½ medium celery root, diced	salt to taste

Pour water over beef and simmer for ½ hour. Brown vegetables in shortening. Add to soup with salt; simmer for 10 minutes. Add parsley. Serves 4.

QUICK SOUP
POLÉVKA Z VAJEČNÉ JÍŠKY

1 cup chopped soup greens	5 cups water or soup stock
¼ cup butter	salt to taste
¼ cup flour	1 tablespoon chopped chives
2 eggs	1 teaspoon soy sauce

Fry vegetables in butter; add flour, and stir until brown. Add eggs, stir constantly until eggs are set. Add water or stock and mix vigorously. Simmer for 10 minutes. Add salt, chives, and soy sauce. Serves 4 to 5.

RYE BREAD SOUP
CHLEBOVÁ POLÉVKA

1 pound stale rye bread, diced	1 egg yolk, beaten
6 cups water or soup stock	1 cup diced cooked smoked meat (optional)
salt to taste	
½ teaspoon caraway seeds	1 cup sliced frankfurters
½ cup sour cream	(optional)

Simmer bread in water or soup stock for 20 to 30 minutes, or until soft enough to rub through strainer. Add salt, butter, and caraway seeds. Before serving, blend in sour cream and egg yolk. Add smoked meat or frankfurters, if desired. Serves 4 to 6.

SMOKED MEAT SOUP
POLÉVKA Z UZENÉHO MASA

½–1 pound smoked meat	1 tablespoon minced
6 cups boiling water	parsley (optional)
1½ cups shredded kale	¼ cup milk (optional)
or celery	1 egg yolk, beaten
1 chopped onion	(optional)
½ cup uncooked farina	
(or cooked rice or	
barley)	

Put meat into water. If meat is too salty, let cook for a few minutes, then pour water off and replace with fresh boiling water. Add vegetables; simmer for 1½ to 2 hours. Strain soup. Purée vegetables through strainer into soup, add farina, rice, or barley, and simmer for 5 minutes.

Meat can be diced and put back into soup, or sliced and served to 2 persons as a main course with the vegetables or a sauce. Before serving soup, add milk, egg yolk, and/or parsley, if desired; mix in well. Serves 4 to 6.

SUPPER OATMEAL
OVESNÁ KAŠE SLANÁ

2 cups oatmeal	6 tablespoons lard
4 cups water	1 large onion, chopped
salt to taste	

Simmer oatmeal in water with salt and 2 tablespoons of the lard for 25 to 30 minutes, stirring constantly. Fry onion in the remaining lard; pour over oatmeal. Serves 6.

TRIPE SOUP
DRŠŤKOVÁ POLÉVKA

1½ pounds tripe
6 cups water
4 tablespoons flour
¼ teaspoon paprika
4 tablespoons lard
1½ cups sliced vegetables
    (carrot, parsnip,
    celery root, onion)
3 tablespoons butter
    dash of pepper

salt to taste
pinch of marjoram
1 tablespoon minced
    parsley
1 clove garlic, minced
1 cup diced cooked
    smoked meat
    (optional)
1 cup sliced frankfurters
    (optional)

Wash tripe in boiling water and clean well. Simmer in water, salted, until tender (about 2 hours). Remove from stock. Brown flour and paprika lightly in lard; brown vegetables in butter. Add both mixtures to soup. Simmer for 10 to 15 minutes. Cut tripe into narrow strips; return to soup. Add pepper, salt, marjoram, parsley, and garlic. Add the smoked meat or frankfurters, if you like. Serves 4 to 6.

SOUP ACCOMPANIMENTS

DOUGH DROPS
KAPÁNÍ

⅛ cup instantized flour
1 egg
2 tablespoons milk

Beat egg and milk. Add flour; mix until smooth. Pour over a fork into boiling soup. Simmer for 4 minutes. Dough Drops can also be poured over a fork into hot fat and fried until golden. Add to soup before serving.

MEAT DUMPLINGS
KNEDLÍČKY POLÉVKY

Follow the same basic procedure for all of the five recipes below.

Liver Dumplings
Játrové

¼ pound liver, ground or scraped

2 tablespoons butter

dash of salt

dash of pepper

1 egg

½ clove garlic, crushed, or pinch of marjoram

1½ cups (approximately) bread crumbs

Cream butter with salt and egg; add balance of ingredients; mix into a stiff dough. Form into balls, each the size of a walnut. Test dough by boiling just one dumpling at first to make sure it does not fall apart; if dough is not thick enough to adhere, add more bread crumbs and make another test dumpling. Simmer dumplings for 3 to 5 minutes.

Liver Rice
Játrová Rýže

Prepare like Liver Dumplings (above), but thin batter by adding ¼ cup of cool stock. Press dough through a coarse sieve directly into boiling soup. Simmer for about 4 minutes.

Marrow Dumplings
Morkové

¼ pound marrow

1 egg

salt to taste

2 tablespoons milk or cream

dash of mace

1⅓ cups (approximately) bread crumbs

Prepare like Liver Dumplings (above).

Brains Dumplings
Mozečkové

boiling water	1 tablespoon chopped
¼ pound brains	onion
¼ cup butter	½ teaspoon minced
salt to taste	parsley
pepper to taste	1 cup (approximately)
1 egg	bread crumbs

Pour water over brains. Drain and skin. Brown in butter with onion. Cool, then mash well with egg. Proceed as for Liver Dumplings (above).

Ham Dumplings
Šunkové

⅓ cup ground ham or	1 tablespoon milk
smoked meat	⅔ cup (approximately)
2 tablespoons butter	bread crumbs
1 egg	

Prepare like Liver Dumplings (above).

CRUMBLED DOUGH
DROBENÍ

1 egg	1 cup (approximately)
¼ teaspoon salt	instantized flour

Beat egg with salt. Work in enough flour to make very stiff dough. Knead well. Grate on a coarse grater; dry. Simmer in soup for 5 to 8 minutes.

The dough can also be fried in hot shortening until golden, and added to soup before serving.

SOUP PANCAKES (SOUP COLOMBINES)
SVÍTEK DO POLÉVKY

Prepare the pancakes or colombines as directed in the recipes below. When they have cooled, slice them in strips and put into soup, or serve them separately.

Liver Pancakes
Játrovy

2 tablespoons butter	pinch of marjoram (or ½
salt to taste	clove garlic, mashed)
2 eggs, separated	1 tablespoon
⅔ cup ground liver	butter for the
¼ cup milk	2 tablespoons baking
1 cup bread crumbs	bread pan
dash of pepper	crumbs

Cream 2 tablespoons butter thoroughly with salt and egg yolks. Add finely ground liver. Fold in stiffly beaten egg whites and bread crumbs mixed with milk. Grease a cake pan with the tablespoon butter, dust thoroughly with bread crumbs, and fill with batter. Bake in a preheated oven at 350° to a golden brown (about 10 to 20 minutes).

Brains Pancakes
Mozečkový

2 tablespoons butter	⅔ cup bread crumbs
salt to taste	1 tablespoon minced
2 eggs, separated	parsley
¼ pound brains	1 tablespoon
1 tablespoon butter	butter for the
½ onion, chopped	2 tablespoons baking
3 tablespoons milk	bread pan
	crumbs

Clean brains and brown in 1 tablespoon butter with the onion. Mash well. Proceed as in Liver Pancakes, using this mixture in place of ground liver.

Ham Pancakes
Šunkový

3 tablespoons butter	1 tablespoon butter ⎤
2 eggs, separated	⎥ for the
⅓ cup minced ham	2 tablespoons ⎬ baking
3 tablespoons milk	bread ⎥ pan
1 cup bread crumbs	crumbs ⎦
salt to taste	

Prepare like Liver Pancakes (above), but substitute ham for liver.

Biscuit Pancakes
Piškotový

2 eggs, separated	1 tablespoon ⎤ for the
salt to taste	butter ⎥ baking
1 tablespoon minced	2 tablespoons ⎬ pan
parsley	flour ⎦
⅓ cup flour	

Beat egg whites until very stiff. Carefully blend in egg yolks, sprinkled with salt and parsley, 1 at a time. Fold in flour. Bake as directed in Liver Pancakes (above).

Vegetable Pancakes
Zeleninový

2 tablespoons butter,	salt to taste
melted	dash of mace
2 eggs, separated	1 or 2 tablespoons milk
¾ cup cooked vegetables	1 tablespoon ⎤ for the
(cauliflower, kale,	butter ⎥ baking
asparagus, or peas)	2 tablespoons ⎬ pan
⅓ cup instantized flour	flour ⎦

Beat egg whites until very stiff, then blend in egg yolks, 1 at a time. Slowly pour in melted butter, stirring constantly. Fold in flour, then gently blend in salt, mace, milk, and vegetables. Bake as directed in Liver Pancakes (above).

MEATS

BOILED BEEF
HOVĚZÍ VAŘENÉ

1 pound beef (shank or chuck)	salt to taste
	1 large onion
4 cups boiling water	2 stalks fresh parsley

Clean meat and pound it. Put into water with salt, onion, and parsley. Cover. Simmer for 2 to 2½ hours. Serve, sliced, with a sauce and dumplings (see Index) or vegetables. Serves 3 to 4.

LARDED ROAST BEEF
HOVĚZÍ PECÉNÉ PRÍRODNÍ

2 pounds beef (top round)	salt to taste
	dash of pepper
2 ounces bacon	2 cups water
1 large onion, chopped	1 tablespoon flour
¼ cup lard	

Lard meat with ½-inch-thick bacon strips. Fry onion in lard until golden; add meat, brown quickly. Sprinkle with salt and pepper, and add ½ cup of water. Cover, and simmer for about 1 hour. Transfer meat to a preheated 350° oven and cook, uncovered, until tender (1 to 1½ hours). Remove meat from pan. Dust the drippings with flour, stir until brown, add remaining water, simmer for 5 to 10 minutes. Slice meat, return to gravy, serve with dumplings or potatoes. Serves 4 to 6.

LARDED ROAST BEEF WITH SOUR CREAM
HOVĚZÍ PEČENĚ NA SMETANĚ

Prepare like Larded Roast Beef (above), but instead of dusting flour onto drippings, blend 1 tablespoon flour into 1 cup of sour cream and pour into drippings. Add water if needed. Simmer for several minutes. Serves 4 to 6.

GINGER ROAST BEEF
HOVĚZÍ PEČENĚ NA ZÁZVORU

Prepare like Larded Roast Beef (see Index), but omit onion, and lard meat with ½-inch-thick bacon strips rolled lightly in ½ teaspoon ground ginger. Dust another ½ teaspoon ginger over meat. Serves 4 to 6.

MUSTARD ROAST BEEF
HOVĚZÍ PEČENĚ NA HORCICI

Prepare like Larded Roast Beef (see Index), but before serving, add 1 tablespoon mustard to the gravy. Serves 4 to 6.

ROAST BEEF WITH FRANKFURTERS
HOVĚZÍ PEČENĚ S UZENKAMI

2 pounds rump roast	¼ pound butter
2 frankfurters	salt to taste
1 medium onion, chopped	pepper to taste
½ carrot, chopped	2 cups water
½ parsnip, chopped	1 tablespoon flour
¼ celery root, chopped	

Lard meat with frankfurters cut into strips lengthwise. Brown vegetables lightly in butter. Add meat, salt, and pep-

per; brown well. Add 1 cup water. Cover, and roast in a 350°
oven until tender (about 2 hours). Remove meat from pan,
dust drippings with flour, and stir until brown. Add remaining water, simmer for 5 minutes. Rub gravy through strainer;
pour over sliced meat. Serves 4 to 6.

ROAST BEEF ZNOJMO
HOVĚZÍ PEČENĚ ZNOJEMSKÁ

2 pounds rolled rib roast	3 peppercorns
2 ounces bacon	2 allspice
1 medium onion, chopped	1 cup water
½ carrot, chopped	2 tablespoons grated stale
½ parsnip, chopped	rye bread
¼ celery root, chopped	2 pickles, chopped
¼ cup butter	¼ cup red wine
salt to taste	

Lard meat with ½-inch-thick bacon strips. Brown vegetables in butter; add meat, and brown on all sides. Add salt,
seasonings, and water. Cover and roast in a 350° oven until
tender (about 2 hours). Remove meat from pan. Add bread
to pan, mixing well into drippings; simmer for 5 minutes.
Rub gravy through a sieve. Add pickles and wine. Return
meat, which has been sliced, to pan. Serves 4 to 6.

BEEFSTEAKS
BIFTEKY

2 pounds tenderloin of beef	1 tablespoon flour
salt to taste	1 cup water or soup stock
pepper to taste	3 tablespoons butter
6 tablespoons lard	

Cut tenderloin into 6 slices, sprinkle with salt and pepper.
Brown in hot lard about 4 to 5 minutes on each side. Arrange
on a hot serving platter. Skim fat from pan, dust drippings
with flour, stir until brown; add water or stock and bring to a
boil; add butter. Pour gravy over meat. Serves 6.

TOURNEDOS
BIFTEKY S VEJCI

Prepare like Beefsteaks (above). Serve each on a slice of toasted rye bread, and top with a fried egg. Serves 6.

BRAISED BEEF
HOVĚZÍ DUŠENÉ PŘÍRODNÍ

2 pounds beef (brisket
   or round)
¼ pound lard or bacon fat
1 or 2 medium onions,
   chopped

salt to taste
dash of pepper
2 cups water
1 tablespoon flour

Pound meat. Brown onion in fat; add meat, salt, and pepper to it. Brown meat well on both sides. Pour ¾ cup of water over meat, cover, and simmer until tender (about 2 to 2½ hours). When tender, remove meat. Dust drippings with the flour, stir until brown, add the remaining water. Simmer for 5 minutes. Slice meat and return it to the gravy. Serve with noodles, potatoes, rice, or dumplings (see Index). Serves 4 to 6.

BRAISED BEEF WITH TOMATOES AND GREEN PEPPERS
HOVĚZÍ DUŠENÉ S RAJSKÝMI JABLÍČKY A ZELENÝMI PAPRIKAMI

1 medium onion, sliced
¼ pound lard or bacon fat
2 pounds beef
   salt to taste
2 cups water

1 tablespoon flour
½ pound tomatoes, peeled
   and sliced
½ pound green peppers,
   sliced

Fry onion in fat until golden. Add meat and salt; brown on both sides. Pour in ¾ cup of water, cover, and simmer until meat is tender (about 2 to 2½ hours). Remove meat from pot. Dust drippings with flour; stir until brown. Add remaining water, tomatoes, and green peppers. Simmer for 10 to 15 minutes. Slice meat and return it to gravy. Serve with rice, potatoes, or dumplings (see Index). Serves 4 to 6.

BRAISED BEEF WITH VEGETABLES
HOVĚZÍ DUŠENÉ NA ZELENINE

¼ pound lard or bacon fat	2 pounds round or brisket
1 medium onion, sliced	of beef
1 small carrot, sliced	salt to taste
1 parsnip, sliced	dash of pepper
½ celery root, sliced	1 tablespoon flour
	2 cups water

Lightly brown vegetables in fat. Pound meat, add salt and pepper. Brown meat on both sides in fat. Pour over it ¾ cup of water, cover, and simmer until tender (about 2 to 2½ hours). Remove meat from pan. Add flour; stir until brown. Add the remaining water. Simmer for about 5 minutes. Rub gravy through a strainer. Slice meat and return it to gravy. Heat and serve with noodles, potatoes, or dumplings (see Index). Serves 4 to 6.

BRAISED BEEFSTEAK
ROŠTĚNKY DUŠENÉ

4 slices ¾-inch-thick	salt to taste
round steak	dash of pepper
¼ pound lard	2 tablespoons flour
1 large onion, chopped	2 cups water

Pound meat, slash borders. Add salt and pepper; roll in flour. Fry quickly in hot lard on both sides. Remove to a heated platter. Brown onion lightly in fat in the same pan. Return meat to pan, add water. Cover, and simmer until tender (30 to 45 minutes), stirring frequently. Serves 4.

BRAISED BEEFSTEAK WITH MUSTARD
RŎSTĔNKY NA HOŘČICI

Prepare like Braised Beefsteak (above), but before serving, add 3 teaspoons prepared mustard to the gravy. Serves 4.

BRAISED BEEFSTEAK WITH ANCHOVIES
ROŠTĔNKY NA SARDELI

Prepare like Braised Beefsteak (above), but use less salt. Before serving, add 2 finely chopped anchovies and 1 tablespoon capers to gravy. Serves 4.

BRAISED BEEFSTEAK WITH VEGETABLES
AND SOUR CREAM
ROŠTĔNKY DUŠENÉ NA ZELENINĔ
SE SMETANOU

4 slices ¾-inch-thick round steak	3 peppercorns
¼ pound lard	1 allspice
salt to taste	½ bay leaf
2 tablespoons flour	1 cup water
1 medium onion, chopped	1 tablespoon vinegar
½ carrot, chopped	1 cup sour cream
½ parsnip, chopped	1 tablespoon flour
¼ celery root, chopped	¼ cup white wine

Pound steak, slash borders. Sprinkle with salt; roll in 2 tablespoons flour. Fry quickly on both sides in half the fat. Brown vegetables lightly in remaining fat; add peppercorns, allspice, bay leaf, water, vinegar, and meat. Simmer until tender (30 to 45 minutes). Remove the meat from pan. Mix sour cream with 1 tablespoon flour; pour into the gravy and blend well. Simmer for 5 minutes. Strain. Return meat to pan and add wine. Serve with dumplings (see Index), potatoes, noodles, or rice. Serves 4.

ROLLED BEEFSTEAKS
ZÁVITKY Z ROŠTĚNEK

4 slices ¾-inch-thick
    round steak
salt to taste
pepper to taste
¼ pound sliced bacon
2 pickles, chopped

⅔ cup chopped cooked
    smoked meat or ham
1 tablespoon flour
3 tablespoons lard
1 medium onion, chopped
2 cups water

Pound meat, slash borders. Sprinkle with salt and pepper. Cover each steak with sliced bacon. Mix pickles and ham; spread over bacon. Roll meat, fasten with skewers or toothpicks. Dust with flour. Brown well in lard. Remove meat, add onion to pan, fry until yellow. Return meat to pan, add 1 cup of water, cover, and simmer until tender (about 1 hour), adding more water as it evaporates. Remove skewers or toothpicks before serving. Serves 4.

VIENNESE BEEFSTEAK
ROŠTĚNKY VÍDEŇSKÉ

4 slices ¾-inch-thick
    top round
salt to taste
pepper to taste
2 tablespoons flour

½ cup lard
1 cup water or soup stock
¼ cup butter
1 large onion, sliced

Pound steaks, slash borders. Dust with salt, pepper, and 1 tablespoon flour. Fry in ¼ cup of the lard, about 4 minutes on each side. Remove to a warm serving dish. Skim off lard in pan; dust with remaining flour; stir until brown. Add water. Bring to a boil, add butter. Pour over meat. Fry onion rings in the rest of the lard and arrange on top of meat. Serves 4.

TENDERLOIN WITH VEGETABLES
SVÍČKOVÁ NA ZELENINĚ

3 pounds tenderloin of beef	salt to taste
3 ounces bacon	1 cup boiling water
2 cups sliced vegetables	5 peppercorns
(onion, carrot,	2 allspice
parsnip, celery root)	1 bay leaf
¼ cup butter	pinch of thyme
	1 tablespoon flour

Lard meat with ½-inch-thick bacon strips. Brown vegetables in butter, add meat, and brown on all sides. Pour in ½ cup of water, salt, and seasonings. Roast in a 325° oven until tender (1 to 1½ hours), basting frequently. Remove meat from pan, dust drippings with flour, stir until brown. Add remaining water and simmer for 5 minutes. Rub gravy through a strainer and pour over sliced meat. Serves 4 to 6.

TENDERLOIN WITH SOUR CREAM
SVÍČKOVÁ NA SMETANĚ

Prepare like Tenderloin with Vegetables (above), but before serving, blend 1 cup of sour cream into gravy. Serves 4 to 6.

TARTAR BEEFSTEAK
BIFTEK TATARSKÝ

1 pound beef tenderloin	3 egg yolks
salt to taste	1 large onion, sliced
pepper to taste	

Skin tenderloin. Chop meat very fine, add salt and pepper. Shape into 3 patties. Make a small indentation in the center of each and drop in an egg yolk. Decorate with onion rings. Serve raw with rolls or dark bread and an assortment of seasonings like paprika, freshly ground pepper, mustard, pickle, relishes, anchovies, or more onion. Serves 3.

BEEF GOULASH
HOVĚZÍ GULÁŠ

2 pounds beef (shank or
    chuck)
¼ cup lard
1 large onion, chopped
¼ teaspoon paprika
    dash of pepper

pinch of marjoram
salt to taste
1 clove garlic, mashed
1 tablespoon flour
2 cups (approximately)
    water

Fry onion in lard until yellow; add paprika and meat; brown. Add seasonings; pour in ½ cup water. Cover, and simmer until tender, adding more water as it evaporates. When meat is done, uncover it, and let all of the water evaporate. Dust with flour; stir until brown. Add 1 cup more water; simmer for 10 to 15 minutes longer. Serves 4 to 6.

BEEF GOULASH WITH PICKLES
HOVĚZÍ GULÁŠ ZNOJEMSKÝ

Prepare like Beef Goulash (above), but during the last 5 minutes of cooking, add 2 finely chopped pickles. Serves 4 to 6.

BEEF GOULASH WITH TOMATOES
AND GREEN PEPPERS
HOVĚZÍ GULÁŠ S RAJČATY
A ZELENYMI PAPRIKAMI

Prepare like Beef Goulash (above), but during the last 10 minutes of cooking, add ½ pound cleaned green peppers cut into strips, and ½ pound peeled sliced tomatoes. Serves 4 to 6.

MUTTON WITH MARJORAM
SKOPOVÉ MASO S MAJORÁNKOU

1½ pounds shoulder of
    mutton, cubed
¾ cup sliced vegetables
    (onion, carrot,
    parsnip, celery root)
6 tablespoons butter

salt to taste
1 or 2 cloves garlic,
    crushed
½ teaspoon marjoram
2 cups water
3 tablespoons flour

Fry vegetables in 3 tablespoons of butter; add meat, salt, garlic, and marjoram; brown well. Add 1 cup water, cover, and simmer until tender (1½ to 2 hours). Brown flour in remaining butter, add rest of water, and bring to a boil; add to meat. Simmer for 5 minutes. Serves 4 to 6.

LEG OF MUTTON WITH SOUR CREAM
SKOPOVÁ KÝTA NA SMETANĚ

2 pounds leg of mutton,
    boned
salt to taste
½ cup sliced vegetables
    (carrot, parsnip,
    celery root)
1 medium onion, chopped
¼ cup lard
2 cups water

5 peppercorns
3 allspice
½ bay leaf
    dash of thyme
1 tablespoon flour
1 cup sour cream
    vinegar or lemon juice
    to taste

Fry vegetables and onion in lard; add meat, brown on all sides. Pour in 1 cup of water, add seasonings; cover and simmer for 1 hour. Remove cover, add remaining water, and roast in a 350° oven for 30 to 45 minutes. Remove meat from pan. Mix flour with sour cream, add to pan juices, simmer for 5 minutes. Strain gravy; add vinegar or lemon juice. Serves 6.

MUTTON WITH CARROTS
SKOPOVÉ MASO S MRKVÍ

1½ pounds shoulder of
    mutton, cubed
    salt to taste
1 medium onion,
    chopped
⅓ cup butter

1½ cups water
1 clove garlic,
    crushed
2 tablespoons flour
1–1½ pounds carrots,
    sliced

Sprinkle meat with salt. Fry onion in butter; add meat, and brown. Pour in ½ cup of water and garlic; cover, and simmer until tender (1½ to 2 hours). Remove meat from pot. Dust drippings with flour, stir until brown; add remaining water. Bring to a boil, add carrots, simmer 10 to 15 minutes (or until tender). Serves 4 to 6.

MUTTON GOULASH
SKOPOVÝ GULÁŠ

1½ pounds shoulder or
    leg of mutton, cubed
1 carrot, chopped
1 parsnip, chopped
½ celery root, chopped
1 onion, chopped
½ cup chopped bacon
    salt to taste
3 cups water
1 clove garlic, crushed

dash of pepper
dash of paprika
¼ teaspoon marjoram
¼ teaspoon caraway
    seeds
1 cup kale, cut in strips
1 cup cut green beans
1 pound potatoes, peeled
    and quartered

Sauté carrot, parsnip, celery root, and onion with the bacon. Add meat, sprinkled with salt, and 1 cup water. Cover, and simmer for 1½ hours. Add seasonings, kale, beans, and potatoes, and the remaining water. Cover, and simmer for 30 to 45 minutes longer. Serves 4 to 6.

MUTTON PILAF
SKOPOVÝ PILAV

1 pound shoulder or leg of mutton, cut into small cubes	¼ teaspoon paprika
	¼ teaspoon caraway seeds
	dash of ginger
1 medium onion, chopped	1 cup long-grained rice
¼ cup butter	¼ cup grated Parmesan cheese
3 cups water	
salt to taste	

Fry onion in butter; add meat, and brown. Add 1 cup water and seasonings. Cover and simmer for 1 to 1½ hours. Add rice and remaining water; simmer, covered, 20 minutes longer. Before serving, sprinkle with cheese. Serves 3 to 4.

ROLLED BREAST OF VEAL
WITH FRANKFURTERS
TELECÍ HRUDÍ JAKO RULÁDA S PÁRKY

2 pounds boned breast of veal	8 frankfurters
salt to taste	3 ounces butter
1 teaspoon paprika	1 cup water
	1 tablespoon flour

Pound breast of veal lightly; sprinkle with salt on both sides. Sprinkle paprika on one side and arrange frankfurters on top; roll up meat and tie. Brown on all sides in melted butter; pour in ⅓ cup water, and roast in a 350° oven for about 2 hours. Remove meat from pan. Mix flour in the remaining water, add to drippings; simmer for 5 to 10 minutes. Slice meat, and serve, either hot with gravy, or cold (without gravy), with salads. Serves 4 to 6.

VEAL CUTLETS WITH MUSHROOMS
TELECÍ ŘÍZKY NA HOUBÁCH

Prepare like Veal Cutlets (below). Before serving, add ½ pound mushrooms sautéed in 1½ teaspoons butter with a pinch of caraway seeds and salt. Serves 4.

VEAL CUTLETS HOLSTEIN
TELECÍ ŘÍZKY HOLŠTÝNSKÉ

Prepare like Veal Cutlets (below). Before serving, add 2 mashed anchovies and 1 teaspoon capers. Serves 4.

PARISIAN VEAL CUTLETS
TELECÍ ŘÍZKY PAŘÍŽSKÉ

1½ pounds leg of veal, cut into 4 slices	3 tablespoons flour
dash of salt	1 tablespoon minced parsley
2 tablespoons flour	1 cup shortening
2 eggs, beaten	2 tablespoons butter
1 tablespoon milk	

Pound meat, sprinkle with salt, dip in flour. Mix eggs, milk, flour, parsley, and dash of salt in a bowl into a smooth batter. Dip meat into batter, then put into hot shortening. Keep moving the pan so cutlets do not stick to it. When batter sets on one side, turn and brown cutlet on the other side; then turn again and brown first side. (This method prevents peeling of crust from meat.) Remove cutlets to platter and spread butter over them. Serves 4.

VEAL CUTLETS
TELECÍ ŘÍZKY PŘÍRODNÍ

1½ pounds leg of veal,
    cut into 4 slices
    salt to taste

2 tablespoons flour
¼ pound butter
½ cup stock or water

Pound meat; sprinkle with salt, dust with flour. Brown quickly in hot butter, 3 to 4 minutes on each side. Remove to a warm platter. Add stock to drippings and bring to a boil. Pour over meat. Serves 4.

VIENNESE VEAL CUTLETS
TELECÍ ŘÍZKY SMAŽENÉ

1½ pounds leg of veal,
    cut into 4 slices
    salt to taste
3 tablespoons flour

2 eggs, beaten
1 cup bread crumbs
½–¾ cup butter
4 lemon wedges

Pound meat; sprinkle with salt. Dip first in flour, then in eggs, then in bread crumbs. Fry in hot butter until golden brown. Serve with lemon wedges. Serves 4.

VEAL GOULASH
DUŠENÉ TELECÍ

1½ pounds shoulder of
    veal, cubed
1 medium onion,
    chopped

6 tablespoons butter
salt to taste
1–1½ cups water or stock
1 tablespoon flour

Brown onion in butter, add meat and salt. Cover pot tightly, and let meat simmer in its own juice for about 1 hour, or until tender. Dust flour over drippings; stir until brown; add water or stock, and simmer for 20 to 30 minutes longer. Serves 4.

VEAL ROAST KARLSBAD
KARLOVARSKÝ KOTOUČ

2½ pounds veal shoulder
salt to taste
¼ pound sliced bacon
4–6 ounces ham, sliced
2–3 eggs, scrambled in
2 tablespoons butter

1 pickle, chopped
6 tablespoons butter
1 tablespoon flour
1½ cups water

Have meat cut in a slice about ¾ inch thick. Pound lightly; sprinkle with salt. Cover with layers of sliced bacon, sliced ham, cooled scrambled eggs, and chopped pickle. Roll up meat and tie tightly. Brown on all sides in butter, add ½ cup water, and roast in a 350° oven for about 1½ to 2 hours, basting frequently. Dust drippings with flour, stir well; add remaining water, simmer for 5 minutes. Serves 6 to 8.

VEAL ROAST WITH WINE
TELECÍ PEČENĚ NA VÍNĚ

2 pounds boned leg of
veal
2 ounces ham
1 pickle
2 ounces bacon
salt to taste
½ cup chopped vegetables
(onion, carrot,
parsnip, celery root)

¼ cup butter
1 cup water
3 peppercorns
1 allspice
1 tablespoon flour
¼ cup white wine

Lard meat with ham, pickle, and bacon. Fry vegetables in butter; add meat, and brown on all sides. Pour in ½ cup of water; add salt, peppercorns, and allspice. Roast in a 325° oven until tender (1½ to 2 hours). Remove meat from pan. Mix flour with remaining water, blend into drippings. Simmer for 5 minutes. Add wine. Strain gravy and serve over sliced meat. Serves 4 to 6.

LARDED VEAL WITH SOUR CREAM
TELECÍ PEČENĚ NA SLANINĚ SE SMETANOU

2 pounds rolled veal roast	1 cup water
3 ounces bacon, cut into	1 tablespoon flour
½-inch-thick strips	1 cup sour cream
¼ cup butter	1 teaspoon lemon juice
salt to taste	

Lard veal with bacon strips, using 2 ounces of the bacon. Chop remaining bacon, fry. Add butter to it, then meat, and brown on all sides. Sprinkle meat with salt, add water, and roast in a 350° oven for about 1½ hours. Baste often. When meat is done, remove from pan. Mix together flour and sour cream, stir into drippings, and simmer for 5 minutes. Slice meat to serve. Before serving, add lemon juice to gravy, and pour over meat. Serves 4 to 6.

STUFFED BREAST OF VEAL
TELECÍ HRUDÍ NADÍVANÉ

3 pounds veal breast	½ cup butter
stuffing	1 tablespoon flour
1 cup water	2 cups water or stock
salt to taste	

Have veal breast boned (reserve bones) and a pocket cut from the large end. Fill about three quarters full with desired stuffing (see recipes below) and sew up the opening. Sprinkle with salt. Melt butter in a roasting pan and brown breast on both sides. Remove from pan. Line up bones in the roasting pan (instead of using a rack), and arrange meat on them; add ½ cup water. Roast in a 350° oven for about 2 hours; baste often. When meat is done, remove from pan together with bones. Dust flour on drippings; stir until brown. Add remaining water, simmer for 5 minutes. Serves 4 to 6.

Roll Stuffing
Nádivka ze žemlí

2 tablespoons diced bacon
2 hard rolls, cut into cubes
2 tablespoons butter, melted
1 cup milk

2 eggs, separated
salt to taste
1 tablespoon minced parsley

Fry bacon, add to rolls with butter and milk, lightly beaten egg yolks, salt, and parsley. Mix well and let stand for about 1 hour. Fold in stiffly beaten egg whites.

Bread Crumb Stuffing
Nádivka ze strouhanky

2 tablespoons butter
2 eggs, separated
salt to taste
5 tablespoons milk

1⅓ cups bread crumbs
2 tablespoons diced bacon, fried

Cream butter, egg yolks, and salt. Pour milk over ⅔ cup of bread crumbs. Add to butter mixture with bacon. Fold in stiffly beaten egg whites and the remaining bread crumbs.

Elbow Macaroni Stuffing
Nádivka z těstovin

½ pound elbow macaroni
3 tablespoons butter
2–3 eggs, separated

salt to taste
1 tablespoon minced parsley
dash of mace

Cook macaroni in 3 quarts salted water for 9 minutes. Drain. Cream butter, add to it egg yolks, salt, parsley, and mace; mix well. Add cooked macaroni. Fold in stiffly beaten egg whites.

VEAL PAPRIKA
TELECÍ MASO NA PAPRICE

1½ pounds shin or
    shoulder of veal,
    cubed
1 medium onion,
    chopped
1 teaspoon paprika
6 tablespoons butter

salt to taste
1 tablespoon flour
1 cup water or stock
2 tomatoes ⎤
1 cup sour ⎬ optional
   cream ⎦

Fry onion and paprika in butter; add meat and salt. Cover, and simmer for about 1 hour. Remove meat from pan. Dust flour onto drippings; stir until brown. Pour in water, and simmer for 5 to 10 minutes. Serves 4 to 6.

VARIATIONS

I. Peel and chop tomatoes; add to pan with meat.
II. Before serving, add sour cream.
III. Add both tomatoes and sour cream.

VEAL AND RICE
RIZOTO

1½ pounds shin or
    shoulder of veal, cut
    into ¾-inch cubes
1 medium onion,
    chopped
6 tablespoons butter
2 tomatoes, peeled and
    cubed

1 cup grated vegetables
    (carrot, parsnip,
    celery root)
1 cup uncooked rice
2 cups water
   salt to taste
⅓ cup grated Parmesan
    cheese

Fry onion in butter; add meat. Cover and simmer for ½ to 1 hour. Add tomatoes and other vegetables, simmer for 10 minutes more. Add rice, sauté 5 to 10 minutes; pour in water, add salt; cover and simmer for 20 to 30 minutes, or until all water is absorbed. Serve with grated Parmesan cheese and a mixed salad. Serves 4 to 6.

BOILED PORK
OVAR

1 pound fresh pork jowl	boiling water to cover
1 pork tongue	salt to taste
1 pork heart	horseradish or mustard
	(optional)

Simmer meats in salted water until tender (about 2 hours). Remove meat from pot. Skin tongue; slice meat. Serve with finely grated horseradish or mustard and rye bread. Serves 4.

QUICK PORK CHOPS OR CUTLETS
VEPŘOVÉ ŘÍZKY NEBO KOTLETY RYCHLÉ

4 pork chops or cutlets,	¼ cup lard
cut ½ inch thick	⅓ cup water
salt to taste	½ teaspoon caraway seeds
1 tablespoon flour	

Pound meat and loosen partially from bone. Dust with salt and flour. Melt lard in an iron skillet and brown meat about 3 minutes on each side. Remove to a warm plate. Skim off half of the lard, add water and caraway seeds to drippings, stir in well, bring to a boil, and serve over meat. Serve with hard rolls or rye bread, and a green salad. Serves 2.

PORK CHOPS WITH MUSHROOMS
NA HŘÍBKÁCH

Prepare like Quick Pork Chops (above). Sauté 1 cup sliced mushrooms in 1 tablespoon butter; add to gravy before serving. Serves 2.

PORK CHOPS WITH CAPERS
NA KAPARECH

Prepare like Quick Pork Chops (above). Before serving, add 1 tablespoon capers. Serves 2.

PORK CHOPS WITH MUSTARD
NA HOŘČICI

Prepare like Quick Pork Chops (above). Before serving, add 1½ teaspoons mustard to gravy. Serves 2.

PORK CHOPS WITH ANCHOVIES
NA SARDELÍCH

Prepare like Quick Pork Chops (above). Before serving, add 2 mashed anchovies to gravy. Serves 2.

BREADED PORK CHOPS OR CUTLETS
VEPŘOVÉ KOTLETY SMAŽENÉ

4 pork chops or cutlets, cut ½ inch thick	1 egg, beaten
salt to taste	⅔ cup bread crumbs
¼ cup flour	¾ cup shortening for frying

Pound meat and partially remove from bone. Sprinkle with salt. Dip first in flour, then in egg; roll in bread crumbs. Fry in hot shortening to a golden brown. Serves 2.

ROAST PORK LOIN
VEPŘOVÁ PEČENĚ

2 pounds end of pork loin   ½ teaspoon caraway
salt to taste   seeds
                                          1⅓ cups water

Sprinkle meat with salt and caraway seeds. Put into a pan, add ⅓ cup water, and roast in a 325° oven for 1½ to 2 hours, basting often and adding water as it evaporates. Serve with dumplings and Sautéed Sauerkraut or Sautéed Cabbage (see Index). Serves 4.

ROAST PORK PIQUANT
VEPŘOVÁ PEČENĚ PIKANTNÍ

2 pounds fresh picnic or   salt to taste
   butt, boned   pepper to taste
2 ounces bacon   ⎱ cut into wedges 2 inches
2 ounces cooked ham   ⎰ long and ¾ inch wide
1 pickle, cut into 2-inch by   1½ cups water
   ½-inch strips   1 carrot, chopped
2 ounces bacon, chopped   1 pickle, chopped
1 medium onion, chopped   1 tablespoon flour

Sprinkle meat with salt and pepper. Cut slits in it big enough to hold the wedges of bacon, ham, and pickle, and push them in. Fry chopped bacon; add onion, let it brown. Add meat, and brown on all sides. Pour in ½ cup water. Cover, and simmer for 45 minutes. Remove cover from pan, add ½ cup water; roast in a 350° oven for 45 minutes. Remove meat from pan, add carrot, chopped pickle, and flour mixed well with remaining ½ cup water. Simmer for 5 minutes. Serve over sliced meat. Serves 4 to 6.

ROAST PORK WITH SOUR CREAM
VEPŘOVÁ PEČENĚ NA SMETANĚ

2 pounds pork tenderloin
    or lean meat from
    leg
salt to taste
pepper to taste
2 ounces bacon cut into
    ½-inch strips

1 medium onion,
    chopped
1 parsnip, chopped
½ celery root, chopped
3 tablespoons butter
1½ cups water
2 tablespoons flour
1 cup sour cream

Sprinkle meat with salt and pepper; lard with bacon strips. Brown vegetables in butter, add meat, and brown well on all sides. Pour in ½ cup water, cover, and simmer for 45 minutes. Remove cover, add ½ cup water, and roast in a 350° oven for 45 minutes. Remove meat from pan. Mix flour with the remaining ½ cup water and sour cream, and stir into drippings. Simmer for 5 minutes. Rub gravy through a sieve, and serve over sliced meat with dumplings (see Index) and cranberries. Serves 4 to 6.

PORK GOULASH
VEPŘOVY GULÁŠ

1½ pounds fresh pork
    shoulder, cubed
1 medium onion,
    chopped
¼ cup lard
¼ teaspoon paprika

½ teaspoon caraway
    seeds
salt to taste
2 cups water
2 tablespoons flour

Fry onion in lard. Add paprika, meat, caraway seeds, and salt; brown well; add ½ cup water; simmer in a covered pan until meat is tender (about 1 hour). Dust drippings with flour; stir until brown. Add remaining water, and simmer for 10 to 20 minutes. Serves 4.

GYPSY GOULASH
CIKÁNSKÝ GULÁŠ

Prepare like Pork Goulash (above). Add 2 peeled, chopped tomatoes and simmer for 5 to 10 minutes. Fry 1 large sliced onion in 1 tablespoon shortening. Serve sprinkled on top of meat. Serves 4.

SEGEDIN GOULASH
SEGEDÍNSKY GULÁŠ

1½ pounds fresh pork shoulder, cubed	salt to taste
1 medium onion, chopped	1 cup water
	½ pound sauerkraut
2 tablespoons shortening	3 tablespoons flour
¼ teaspoon paprika	2 tablespoons lard
½ teaspoon caraway seeds	1 cup sour cream

Fry onion in shortening. Add meat, paprika, caraway seeds, and salt. Brown well. Add ½ cup water, cover, and simmer for 45 minutes. Add two-thirds of the sauerkraut and simmer for 30 minutes longer. Brown flour in lard, stirring well, and add to meat with the remaining water; simmer for 5 minutes. Add sour cream and the remaining sauerkraut. Bring to a boil and serve. Serves 4 to 6.

RAZNICI
RAŽNIČI

1½ pounds tenderloin of pork or lean fresh ham	salt to taste
	¼ cup oil
	1 cup chopped onion

Cut meat into small pieces (about 2½ inches by 2½ inches and ⅜ inch thick), crossgrain. Pound lightly, sprinkle with salt, and brush with oil. Broil on a hot open grill for 6 minutes on each side (or cook in a greased iron skillet). Serve with chopped onion and dark bread. Serves 4 to 6.

MEAT LOAF
SEKANÁ PEČENĚ

1½ pounds ground beef	¾ cup milk
¾ pound ground pork	½ cup diced bacon
salt to taste	1 medium onion,
pepper to taste	chopped
2 eggs	½ cup lard
3 rolls	1 cup stock

Mix meats together, add salt and pepper; add eggs. Soak rolls in milk and squeeze almost dry, then chop them and add to mixture with half the bacon. Fry the rest of the bacon, add onion, and brown. Cool, and add to meat. Mix well. Form into a roll with floured hands. Melt lard in a roasting pan and place meat roll on top. Roast in a 350° oven for 1 to 1½ hours, adding stock as needed and basting frequently. Serves 6 to 8.

MEAT LOAF WITH SOUR CREAM
SEKANÁ PEČENĚ SE SMETANOVOU OMÁČKOU

Prepare like Meat Loaf (above), but instead of lard, use another ¼ cup chopped bacon and another chopped onion. When meat loaf is done, remove from pan. Mix 1 tablespoon flour with 1 cup sour cream, stir into gravy, simmer for 5 minutes, and strain. Serves 6 to 8.

BUFFET MEAT LOAF
SEKANÁ PEČENĚ PLNĚNÁ VEJCI

Prepare like Meat Loaf (above). Shape into a rectangle 2 inches thick on a wooden board sprinkled with bread crumbs. Arrange 3 to 4 hard-cooked eggs with the ends cut off in an unbroken line on top of meat. Roll meat up. Roast like Meat Loaf, or place in a greased loaf pan and roast, covered, in a pan of water. Serve cold with potato or vegetable salad. Serves 6 to 8.

CEVABCICI
ČEVABČIČI

1½ pounds lean pork, ground	pepper to taste
salt to taste	¼ cup flour
	1 cup chopped onion

Mix meat with salt and pepper. Roll in your hands into 2½-inch-long sticks, ¾ inch in diameter. Roll in flour, then broil on a hot open grill until brown. (Or pan fry in a greased iron skillet.) Serve with chopped onion and dark bread. Serves 4 to 6.

FRIED MEAT PATTIES
KARBANÁTKY

¾ pound ground pork	1 tablespoon minced parsley
¾ pound ground beef	1 roll
salt to taste	¼ cup milk
pepper to taste	1 egg white
1 small onion, chopped	1 tablespoon water
1 tablespoon chopped bacon	¾ cup bread crumbs
1 egg	¾ cup shortening

To meat add salt and pepper. Fry onion with bacon. Add to meat with egg and parsley. Soak the roll in milk and squeeze almost dry. Mince, and add to meat mixture. Mix well, and form into patties about 3½ inches in diameter and ¾ inch thick. Brush with egg white beaten with water; roll in bread crumbs. Fry slowly in hot shortening until golden brown. Serves 4 to 6.

VEAL HASLET WITH SOUR CREAM
TELECÍ KOŘÍNEK SE SMETANOU

1½ pounds veal haslet
    (heart, liver, etc.)
    salt to taste
1 medium onion,
    chopped
½ carrot, sliced
½ parsnip, sliced
¼ celery root, sliced
4 peppercorns

2 allspice
    pinch of thyme
½ bay leaf
2 tablespoons lemon
    juice
¼ cup butter
⅓ cup flour
1½ cups stock
½ cup sour cream

Simmer cleaned haslet in salted water to cover with ½ onion, other vegetables, spices, and lemon juice until tender (1½ to 2 hours). Remove meat from pot, cut into thin strips. Fry remaining ½ onion in butter, add flour, and brown. Pour in stock and bring to a boil. Return meat to gravy and simmer for 5 to 10 minutes. Before serving, add sour cream. Serves 3 to 4.

BREADED BEEF BRAIN
HOVĚZÍ MOZEČEK SMAŽENÝ

1 pound beef brain
    salt to taste
½ cup flour

2 eggs, beaten
1 cup bread crumbs
¾ cup shortening

Scald brain and place it in cold water; remove membranes. Slice; sprinkle with salt. Dip slices first in flour, then in eggs, then in bread crumbs; fry in hot shortening until golden brown. Serves 3 to 4.

BREADED VEAL BRAINS
SMAŽENÝ MOZEĆEK

2 veal brains
    salt to taste
⅓ cup flour
2 eggs, lightly beaten

1½ cups bread crumbs
1 cup shortening for
    frying

Clean the brains as in Brains with Eggs (see Index); dry. Cut lengthwise into halves. Salt and roll in flour. Dip in eggs, roll in bread crumbs. Fry in hot shortening until golden brown. Serves 3 to 4.

BRAINS WITH EGGS
MOZEČEK S VEJCI

2 veal brains	1 teaspoon minced
⅓ cup butter	parsley
1 small onion, chopped	salt to taste
4 eggs, beaten	

Wash brains in cold water. Place in a sieve and dip first in boiling water, then in cold water; remove membranes. Break brains into small pieces. Sauté onion in butter, add brains, and cook (about 15 to 20 minutes). Add eggs and continue to cook over low heat, stirring constantly, until mixture begins to set. Add parsley and salt before serving. Serves 4.

BRAISED BEEF KIDNEYS
DUŠENÉ HOVĚZÍ LEDVINKY

1½ pounds beef kidneys	¼ teaspoon caraway
1 onion, chopped	seeds
¼ cup shortening	1 tablespoon flour
dash of pepper	1 cup water or soup stock
	salt to taste

Split kidneys lengthwise; remove outer and inner membranes, and slice. Wash and drain about 3 times; place on absorbent paper. Fry onion in hot shortening, add kidney slices, pepper, and caraway seeds; brown. Cover, and let dish simmer in its own juices until tender (10 to 20 minutes). Dust with flour, stir until brown; add stock, and simmer 5 minutes longer. Add salt just before serving. Serves 3 to 4.

QUICK PORK KIDNEYS
VEPŘOVÉ LEDVINKY NARYCHLO

1½ pounds kidneys
1 medium onion, chopped
¼ cup lard
¼ teaspoon caraway seeds

dash of pepper
1 tablespoon flour
⅔ cup water
salt to taste

Split kidneys lengthwise. Remove inner and outer membranes. Wash well under running water and pat dry. Slice. Fry onion in lard, add kidney slices, caraway seeds, and pepper; brown for about 7 minutes or until done. Remove meat from pan. Dust drippings with flour and stir until brown; add water. Bring to a boil, stir in salt; serve gravy over kidneys. Serves 3 to 4.

BRAISED SWEETBREADS
BRZLÍK DUŠENÝ

1 pair sweetbreads
1 tablespoon chopped bacon
1 small onion, chopped
salt to taste

pepper to taste
1 cup vegetable stock or water
2 teaspoons flour

Wash sweetbreads in cold water. Simmer for 5 minutes in boiling salted water; drain. Plunge into cold water, slip off the thin membrane, and cut out thick connective tissue and fat. Break into small pieces. Put bacon into hot frying pan, add onion, and brown. Add sweetbreads, salt, and pepper. Brown well. Pour in ½ cup stock and simmer until tender (about 20 minutes). Dust with flour; stir until brown. Add remaining stock and simmer 5 minutes longer. Serves 2.

BREADED SWEETBREADS
BRZLÍK SMAŽENÝ

1 pound sweetbreads	1½ cups bread crumbs
salt	¾ cup shortening for
⅓ cup flour	frying
2 eggs, slightly beaten	

Clean and simmer sweetbreads as for Braised Sweetbreads (see Index). Pat dry and split into halves lengthwise. Roll in flour, dip in eggs, then roll in bread crumbs. Fry in hot shortening to a golden brown. Serve with Tartar Sauce (see Index). Serves 3 to 4.

BRAISED VEAL HEART
TELECÍ SRDCE DUŠENÉ

2 veal hearts	pepper to taste
¼ pound bacon	2 tablespoons flour
¼ cup butter	1 cup water or stock
1 medium onion, chopped	¼ cup white wine
salt to taste	

Clean veal hearts, slice, and lard with bacon strips. Dust with flour, salt, and pepper. Fry onion in butter, add meat; brown. Pour in stock and simmer until tender (about 1 to 1½ hours). Add wine to gravy before serving. Serves 4.

BREADED CALF'S LIVER
TELECÍ JÁTRA SMAŽENÁ

1½ pounds calf's liver,	2 eggs, beaten
sliced ½ inch thick	1 cup bread crumbs
salt to taste	¾ cup shortening
2 tablespoons flour	

Pound liver lightly; sprinkle with salt. Dip first in flour, then in beaten eggs; roll in bread crumbs. Fry in hot shortening until golden brown. Serves 4.

LARDED CALF'S LIVER
TELECÍ JÁTRA NA SLANINĚ

1½ pounds calf's liver, sliced	dash of pepper
2 ounces bacon	3 tablespoons flour
salt to taste	¼ cup butter or lard
	½ cup stock or water

Lard sliced liver with bacon. Dust with salt, pepper, and 2 tablespoons flour. Brown in hot fat (about 3 minutes on each side). Remove to a warm platter, dust drippings with remaining flour; stir until brown. Add stock, simmer for 3 minutes; pour over liver. Serves 6.

PÂTÉ SPICE
PAŠTIKOVÉ KOŘENÍ

20 peppercorns	pinch of thyme
14 allspice	1 bay leaf
pinch of ginger	

Grind or pound all spices in a mortar, and sift through a fine sieve or whirl in the blender. Keep in a tightly closed jar. This may also be purchased already prepared. (See Explanatory Notes.)

GOOSE LIVER WITH WINE
HUSÍ JÁTRA S VÍNEM

1 goose liver (½ pound)	2 tablespoons Madeira wine
2 tablespoons flour	salt to taste
¼ cup lard	1 tablespoon butter
1 medium onion, chopped	

Slice liver and roll in flour; brown in lard. Add onion, cover, and sauté until tender (about 10 minutes). Remove liver from pan; skim off fat, add wine, and bring to a boil. Before serving, sprinkle liver with salt, and add butter to gravy. Serves 2.

GOOSE OR DUCK LIVER WITH ONIONS
JÁTRA NA CIBULCE

½ pound liver (goose or
    duck)
1 tablespoon chopped
    onion
4 tablespoons lard

½ teaspoon caraway seeds
1 tablespoon flour
¼ cup water
    salt to taste
1 large onion, sliced

Wilt chopped onion in 2 tablespoons lard. Add liver and caraway seeds. Cook for 8 to 10 minutes on each side. Dust with flour; brown. Pour water into pan and bring to a boil. Add salt just before serving. Fry onion slices in remaining lard and use as garnish for liver. Serves 2.

GOOSE LIVER PÂTÉ
HUSÍ PAŠTIKA JEMNÁ

1 pound goose liver
1 cup milk
½ cup chopped bacon
½ teaspoon Pâté Spice
    (see Index)
¼ teaspoon pepper

1 tablespoon Madeira
    wine, rum, or cognac
2 egg yolks
    salt to taste
½ pound bacon, sliced

Soak liver in milk for a few hours. Remove membranes. Slice one third of the liver thinly, and grind remaining liver twice. Add chopped bacon, spices, and wine. Add egg yolks and salt, and mix well. Line a loaf pan or a covered pudding form with bacon slices. Fill with alternate layers of ground liver and sliced liver, starting and ending with ground liver. Cover with rest of bacon slices. The form should not be more than three quarters full. Cover (use foil to cover loaf pan), and simmer for 2 hours in a large pan of boiling water reaching halfway up the form. Cool before unmolding.

PORK LIVER PÂTÉ
PAŠTIKA Z VEPŘOVYCH JATER

½ pound pork liver
½ pound potatoes, cooked
 and cooled
1 small onion, chopped
½ tablespoon lard
2 eggs

salt to taste
pepper to taste
Pâté Spice
 (see Index)
⅓ cup diced bacon
2 tablespoons lard

Remove membranes from liver. Fry onion in lard. Grind liver and onions very fine (or twice) with potatoes. Add eggs, seasonings, and bacon. Beat well. Cook like Veal Liver Pâté (below), 1 to 1½ hours.

PÂTÉ FROM LEFTOVER MEAT
PAŠTIKA ZE SBYTKŮ MASA

Prepare like Veal Liver Pâté (below), using any leftover roast or boiled meat, and an equal amount of veal or pork liver.

VEAL LIVER PÂTÉ
PAŠTIKA Z TELECÍCH JATER

1 small onion, chopped
½ cup chopped bacon
½ pound pork, cubed
1 pound veal liver
1 roll
½ cup milk
2 eggs
 salt to taste

pepper to taste
dash of Pâté Spice (see
 Index)
2 tablespoons red wine or
 ¼ teaspoon rum
2 tablespoons lard, or
 bacon slices

Fry onion with bacon. Add pork, cover, and simmer until tender. Remove membranes from liver. Grind very fine (or twice) with cooked meat and the roll, which has been soaked in milk. Add eggs, seasonings, and wine or rum. Beat mixture well. With the lard, grease a loaf pan or a covered pudding form which has smooth sides, or line it with slices of bacon. Pour in mixture (pan should be three quarters full). Put into a large pot with water coming to within one third of the top of the form, cover (use foil to cover loaf pan), and simmer for 1 to 1½ hours. Cool overnight in the refrigerator before un-molding. Serve in ½-inch-thick slices. Serves 6.

LIVER SAUSAGE FILLING
JITRNICOVÝ PRÝT

2 pounds meat from pig's head
¼ pound pork liver
2 rolls
¼ teaspoon marjoram
dash of pepper
dash of ground allspice

1 large clove of garlic, mashed
dash of ginger
salt to taste
½ cup stock
1 tablespoon lard

Simmer meat in salted water until tender (1 to 1½ hours). Soak the rolls in stock and squeeze almost dry. Chop together meat, raw liver, and rolls, or grind coarsely. Add spices, garlic, salt, and stock. Mix well, pour into a greased pan, and bake in a 375° oven for 45 minutes. Serve hot with potatoes and sauerkraut, or cold with dark bread. Serves 6 to 8.

BOILED SMOKED BEEF TONGUE
HOVĚZÍ JAZYK UZENÝ VAŘENÝ

1 smoked beef tongue
boiling water

Place tongue in boiling water and simmer until tender (2 to 4 hours). Remove to cold water; skin. Slice, and serve hot or cold, with a sauce, vegetables, or salads.

BOILED BEEF TONGUE
HOVĚZÍ JAZYK VAŘENÝ

1 fresh beef tongue (about
    4 pounds)
1 medium onion
1 carrot
1 parsnip

water to cover
salt
½ celery root
beaten egg ⎫ optional
bread crumbs ⎭

Simmer tongue in salted water until tender (3 to 4 hours). Add vegetables during last ½ hour of cooking. Remove tongue from pot, place it in cold water, and skin. Slice, and serve with Anchovy or Polish Sauce (see Index), or fry the pieces, dipped first in beaten egg and then in bread crumbs. Reserve stock for use in sauces or roasting. Serves 6.

JELLIED BRAWN
VEPŘOVÁ HUSPENINA (SULC)

1½ pounds meat from pig's
    head
1 pork tongue
2 hocks
½ pound skin
    water to cover meats
    salt to taste

1 medium onion
1 carrot
1 parsnip
½ celery root
6 peppercorns
½ cup vinegar

Clean meat. Simmer with tongue in salted water for 1 hour. Add vegetables, peppercorns, and vinegar, and simmer for 1 hour longer. Remove from pot. Dice meat; put into a deep bowl. Skin tongue, dice it, and add to meat. Return skin and bones to stock, simmer for 1 hour. Drain, skim off fat; pour stock over meat. Let it set in refrigerator, then turn out onto a plate and slice. Serve with finely chopped onion, vinegar or lemon juice, and dark bread. Serves 6 to 8.

ROASTED BEEF TONGUE
WITH ANCHOVY BUTTER
HOVĚZÍ JAZYK PEČENÝ
SE SARDELOVÝM MÁSLEM

1 fresh beef tongue, boiled and skinned (see above)	1 medium onion, chopped
	½ teaspoon lemon juice
	1 cup stock
¼ pound butter	1 cup bread crumbs
6 anchovies, mashed	

Cream half the butter with anchovies; spread over cooked tongue. Brown onion in the remaining butter, add meat; brown. Pour in ½ cup stock. Roast in a 350° oven for about 1 hour or until tongue is brown on both sides. Sprinkle with lemon juice and bread crumbs, add remaining stock, and bake until bread crumbs are golden brown. Serves 6.

CREAMED TRIPE
ZADĚLÁVANÉ DRŠŤKY

3 pounds tripe	2 cups (approximately) stock
1 medium onion	
1 carrot	dash of pepper
1 parsnip	dash of marjoram
½ celery root	1 clove garlic, mashed
salt	1 cup diced, cooked, smoked meat or ham
½ cup flour	
¼ pound lard or butter	1 tablespoon chopped parsley
½ teaspoon paprika	

Wash tripe thoroughly in scalding water and clean well. Simmer in salted water until tender (about 2 hours). During the last ½ hour add vegetables. Strain; cool tripe. Brown flour in lard or butter and add paprika. Pour in stock, a little at a time, stirring constantly to make a smooth sauce. Add seasonings, and simmer for 10 to 15 minutes. Cut tripe in thin strips and put into sauce with diced smoked meat and parsley. Serve with onion or salt rolls. Serves 6 to 8.

POULTRY AND GAME

ROAST STUFFED CHICKEN
NADÍVANÉ KUŘE PEČENÉ

1 roasting chicken (3—4
    pounds)
salt to taste
¼ cup butter

1 recipe Bread Crumb
    Stuffing (see below)
1 cup water

Clean and stuff the chicken. Sprinkle with salt and rub with butter, and add any remaining butter to roasting pan. Roast bird in 350° oven for 45 to 60 minutes. Baste frequently with water, adding it as needed. Serves 4 to 5.

Bread Crumb Stuffing
Nádivka

½ cup butter
3 eggs, separated
1 chicken liver, chopped
1⅓ cups bread crumbs

½ cup light cream or milk
salt to taste
1 tablespoon minced
    parsley

Cream butter; add egg yolks, 1 at a time, blending in thoroughly. Mix in liver, bread crumbs soaked in cream or milk, salt, and parsley. Fold in stiffly beaten egg whites. Pack lightly into cavity of bird.

PARISIAN FRIED CHICKEN
SMAŽENÉ KUŘE V TĚSTÍČKU

1 frying chicken, cut up	⅓ cup flour
dash of salt	2–3 egg whites
2 tablespoons white wine	1 cup shortening
1 teaspoon oil	

Sprinkle chicken with salt. Mix together wine, oil, flour, and salt. Add stiffly beaten egg whites. Dip chicken in this mixture to coat well. Fry to a golden brown. Serves 2 to 3.

CHICKEN FRICASSEE
KUŘE ZADĚLÁVANÉ

1 chicken (3–4 pounds)	1½ cups water
salt to taste	3 tablespoons flour
7 tablespoons butter	½ cup sliced mushrooms
½ carrot	1 tablespoon minced
½ parsnip	parsley
½ celery root	2 tablespoons heavy
1 medium onion	cream
dash of pepper	1 egg yolk
dash of nutmeg	lemon juice to taste
piece of lemon peel	

Sprinkle chicken with salt; brown with vegetables in 3 tablespoons butter. Add spices, lemon peel, and water. Cover, and simmer until tender (about 45 minutes). Remove chicken from pan. Brown flour in 3 tablespoons butter, and stir into pan. Simmer gravy for 5 to 10 minutes; strain over chicken. Add mushrooms browned in 1 tablespoon butter, parsley, and cream, and bring to a boil. Just before serving, blend in egg yolk and lemon juice. Serves 4 to 5.

CHICKEN PAPRIKA
KUŘE NA PAPRICE

1 chicken (3–4 pounds)	½ teaspoon paprika
1 medium onion, chopped	salt to taste
¼ cup chopped bacon or butter	1½ cups water
	½ cup sour cream
	2 tablespoons flour

Cut chicken into small pieces. Wilt onion in bacon or butter, add paprika, chicken, and salt; brown. Add water, cover, and simmer until tender (about 45 minutes). Remove chicken from pan. Mix sour cream with flour, stir carefully into pan; simmer gravy for 5 minutes. Strain over chicken. Serves 4 to 5.

CHICKEN WITH MUSHROOMS
KUŘE S HOUBAMI

1 chicken (3–4 pounds)	salt to taste
½ cup butter	1½ cups water
1 large onion, chopped	1 cup sour cream
1 cup sliced mushrooms	1 tablespoon flour

Cut chicken into small pieces and brown in butter. Add onion; wilt; add mushrooms, salt, and water. Cover, and simmer until tender (about 45 minutes). Remove chicken from pan. Mix sour cream and flour together, blend into pan juices, and bring gravy to a boil. Serve with chicken. Serves 4 to 5.

ROAST CAPON
KAPOUN PEČENÝ

1 capon (5–6 pounds)	1½ cups water
salt to taste	¼ cup butter
¼ cup bacon, cut into strips	

Clean capon, rub with salt. Lard breast and legs with bacon. Put 2 tablespoons butter in roasting pan, add water, and lay in bird. Roast in 325° oven until tender (2½ to 3 hours), turning and basting frequently. Before serving, add the remaining butter. Serves 6 to 8.

ROAST GOOSE
PEČENÁ HUSA

1 8-pound goose	½ teaspoon caraway seeds
salt to taste	2 cups water

Clean and wash goose. Sprinkle with salt and caraway seeds inside and outside. Pour 1 cup water into a roasting pan, put in goose, breast down; cover, and roast in a 375° oven for 1½ hours. Turn goose and roast, uncovered, for 1 hour longer. During the roasting, pierce skin several times, skim off excess fat, and add more water as needed. Serve with dumplings and Sautéed Sauerkraut (see Index). Serves 6 to 8.

ROAST DUCK
PEČENÁ KACHNA

Prepare like Roast Goose (above). Roast in a 350° oven for 1½ to 2 hours. Finish and serve like goose. A 5-pound duck serves 4.

DUCK WITH PEAS
KACHNA S HRÁŠKEM

1 duck	2 tablespoons diced
salt to taste	bacon
2 tablespoons butter	10 small onions, whole
½ cup water	1 pound fresh peas

Cut duck in serving pieces and sprinkle with salt. Sauté in butter until almost tender (about 1 hour). Add water as needed. Add bacon, onions, and peas, and cook until vegetables are tender (about 20 minutes). Serves 4.

ROAST TURKEY WITH STUFFING
PEČENÝ KROCAN S NÁDIVKOU

1 turkey (14–16 pounds)	salt to taste
White Bread Stuffing	½ cup butter
(see below)	water as needed

Clean turkey; stuff body and neck cavities, and close with skewers, or sew up. Sprinkle with salt and rub with butter. Roast in a 325° oven for 5¼ to 6 hours. Add water as needed; baste frequently.

White Bread Stuffing
Žemlová nádivka

¾ cup chopped bacon	½ cup minced parsley
¾ cup butter	¼ teaspoon nutmeg or
2 cups milk	mace
3–4 eggs, lightly beaten	10 cups soft white diced
salt to taste	bread

Melt bacon, add butter. Mix milk with eggs, salt, and seasonings. Add melted fat and beat well. Pour over diced bread. Let stand ½ hour, stirring often so that all the liquid is absorbed.

White Bread Stuffing with Almonds
S mandlemi

Prepare White Bread Stuffing (above). Add ½ cup blanched, chopped almonds.

White Bread Stuffing with Chestnuts
S kaštany

Prepare White Bread Stuffing (above). Add 1 cup cooked, chopped chestnuts.

Meat Stuffing
Masitá nádivka

¼ pound veal, ground
¼ pound pork, ground
¼ pound cooked, smoked
    meat, ground
    turkey liver, ground
1½ cups diced rolls
⅔ cup milk

¼ cup butter, melted
2 eggs, lightly beaten
    salt to taste
    pepper to taste
2 anchovies, mashed
¼ teaspoon lemon peel

Sprinkle milk over rolls. Mix all ingredients well.

STUFFED ROAST SQUAB
HOLOUBATA S NÁDIVKOU

3 squabs
    salt to taste

¼ cup butter
1 cup water

STUFFING

¼ cup butter
2 eggs, separated
    salt to taste
    chopped livers
1¼ cups bread crumbs

¼ cup milk
    dash of mace
1 tablespoon minced
    parsley

Clean squabs; loosen skin from breasts. Stuff body and neck cavities (see below), and tie with thread. Sprinkle with salt and rub with butter. Melt any remaining butter in roasting pan, lay in squabs, and roast in a 325° oven for 30 to 45 minutes, adding water as needed. Remove thread before serving.

To prepare stuffing, cream butter thoroughly with egg yolks and salt. Add livers, bread crumbs soaked in milk, and seasonings. Mix well. Fold in stiffly beaten egg whites. Pack lightly into cavities. Serves 3.

HUNTER'S SQUAB
HOLUBI NA DIVOKO

2 squabs
½ cup bacon cut into strips
  salt to taste
1 medium onion,
  chopped
3 tablespoons butter

¼ cup celery root
4 peppercorns
3 allspice
2 cloves
1 cup water (as needed)
1 tablespoon flour

Clean squabs; lard breasts with bacon. Sprinkle with salt; truss. Fry onion in butter, add squabs to pan, add seasonings and a little water. Cover, and cook until tender (30 to 45 minutes). Remove squabs from pan, dust drippings with flour, stir until brown, add ½ cup water. Simmer for 5 minutes. Strain gravy. Serves 2.

ROAST PHEASANT
PEČENÝ BAŽANT

1 pheasant
¾ cup bacon cut into
  ½-inch strips
  salt to taste
1 small onion, chopped

5 peppercorns
½–1 cup water (as
  needed)

Clean pheasant; lard with half the bacon. Rub with salt. Melt the remaining bacon and wilt onion in it. Place pheasant on it, and roast in a 375° oven 1 to 1½ hours. Add water as needed. Serves 3 to 4.

ROAST PARTRIDGE
KOROPTVE PEČENÉ

2 partridges
  salt to taste
2 ounces bacon, sliced
½ small onion, chopped

¼ cup butter
1 cup water
3 peppercorns
1 juniper berry

Clean partridges; sprinkle with salt. Wrap in thin slices of bacon; tie. Cook onion in butter until soft. Add partridges, brown on both sides. Pour in ½ cup water, add spices. Roast in a 375° oven for 45 minutes. Baste frequently. Remove meat from pan, skim off fat. Add remaining water and bring to a boil. Strain gravy. Serves 2.

RABBIT PAPRIKA
KRÁLÍK NA PAPRICE

1 rabbit	1 teaspoon paprika
salt to taste	2 cups water
1 large onion, chopped	2 tablespoons flour
6 tablespoons butter	1 cup sour cream

Clean rabbit, cut into serving pieces, and sprinkle with salt. Fry onion in butter, add paprika and meat, and brown on all sides. Pour in water; cover and simmer until tender (about 1 hour). Remove meat from pan. Mix flour with sour cream, add to gravy, and simmer for 5 minutes. Serves 6 to 8.

ROAST HARE WITH SOUR CREAM
ZAJÍC NA SMETANĚ

1 hare rump	1½ cups water
salt to taste	8 peppercorns
4 ounces bacon, cut in	4 allspice
½-inch strips	1 bay leaf
1 cup diced vegetables	dash of thyme
(carrot, parsnip,	strip of lemon peel
celery root)	2 tablespoons flour
1 large onion, chopped	2 cups sour cream
½ cup butter	lemon juice to taste

Remove membranes from hare, clean, and salt. Lard with bacon. Fry vegetables and onion in butter, add meat, and brown on both sides. Pour in water, spices, and lemon peel; roast in a 325° oven until tender (about 1½ hours). Remove meat from pan and cut into serving pieces. Mix flour with sour cream, add to pan, blend well. Simmer gravy for 5 minutes; rub through a sieve, add lemon juice. Serves 4 to 6.

HARE WITH BLACK SAUCE
ZAJÍC NA ČERNO

1 hare forepart, cut up
lungs and heart, cut
  into serving pieces
¼ pound bacon, chopped
5 tablespoons butter
1 large onion, chopped
  salt to taste
6 peppercorns

3 allspice
1 bay leaf
  dash of thyme
  strip of lemon peel
2½ cups water
3 tablespoons flour
1 teaspoon sugar
  juice of 1 lemon

Fry bacon, add to it onion and 2 tablespoons of butter; brown. Add meat, salt, seasonings, and lemon peel. Cover. Simmer first in its own juice; then add water as necessary and simmer until tender (1 to 1½ hours). Pour off juices; strain. Brown flour in remaining butter, pour in pan juices, and simmer, stirring gently, until thickened. Melt sugar in a skillet until brown. Add to gravy. Add lemon juice. Serves 4.

ROAST LEG OR SADDLE OF VENISON
SRNČÍ KÝTA NEBO HŘBET PEČENÝ

2 pounds boned leg or
  saddle of venison
4 ounces bacon, cut into ½-
  inch strips
6 tablespoons butter,
  melted

1 medium onion, chopped
  salt to taste
2 juniper berries
2 cups water
1 tablespoon flour

Wipe meat with a damp cloth. Remove membranes. Lard with bacon. Brush melted butter over meat; refrigerate 1 to 2 days. To cook, scrape butter off meat, and melt it. Add onion, and cook until soft. Sprinkle meat with salt; add to onion, brown on all sides. Add juniper berries and 1 cup water. Cover, and simmer for 30 minutes. Remove cover, and roast meat in a 350° oven until tender (30 to 40 minutes). Remove meat from pan. Mix flour and remaining water together and pour into drippings; simmer for 5 minutes. Strain sauce, and serve with venison. Serves 4 to 6.

LEG OF VENISON WITH RED WINE
SRNČÍ MASO S ČERVENÝM VÍNEM

2 pounds leg of venison, boned	2 cups water
4 ounces bacon, cut in ½-inch strips	4 peppercorns
salt to taste	2 allspice
¾ cup sliced vegetables (parsnip, celery root, carrot)	½ bay leaf
	strip of lemon peel
1 medium onion, chopped	1 tablespoon flour
5 tablespoons butter	½ teaspoon sugar
	lemon juice to taste
	¼ cup red wine

Lard meat with bacon and sprinkle with salt. Fry vegetables and onion in butter, add meat, and brown on all sides. Pour in 1 cup of water, add spices and lemon peel; simmer until tender (about 1 hour). Remove meat from pot. Mix flour with remaining cup of water, add to drippings, and simmer for 5 minutes. Add sugar, lemon juice, and wine. Rub through a sieve. Serves 4 to 6.

LEG OF VENISON WITH SOUR CREAM
SRNČÍ NA SMETANĚ

Prepare like Venison with Red Wine (above), but instead of red wine, add 2 cups sour cream mixed with 2 tablespoons flour. Simmer for 5 minutes. Serves 4 to 6.

FISH

CARP WITH BLACK SAUCE
KAPR NA ČERNO

3 pounds carp
½ cup vinegar
salt to taste
2 cups diced vegetables
(celery root, carrot,
parsnip)
1 large onion, chopped
¼ cup butter
½ cup grated stale rye
bread
½ cup grated gingerbread
6 peppercorns
3 allspice

½ bay leaf
dash of thyme
piece of lemon peel
1 cup red wine
3 tablespoons vinegar
water as needed
1 tablespoon prune butter
1 tablespoon currant jam
½ cup raisins
½ cup sliced Blanched
Almonds (see Index)
lemon juice to taste

Carp is traditionally served on Christmas Eve.

Wash carp, and rinse in the ½ cup vinegar. Cut into serving pieces and sprinkle with salt. Brown vegetables and onions in butter. Add rye bread, gingerbread, and seasonings. Pour in wine and the 3 tablespoons vinegar. Stir. If gravy is too thick, add a little water. Simmer for 15 minutes. Add carp, simmer for 15 minutes more. Remove fish from pot. Strain gravy, and to it add prune butter, currant jam, raisins, almonds, and lemon juice. Simmer for 5 minutes. Return carp to gravy. This tastes best served next day. Serve with dumplings (see Index). Serves 4 to 6.

BLUE CARP
KAPR NA MODRO

3 pounds carp
3 cups water
  salt to taste
1 cup sliced vegetables
  (celery root, parsnip,
  carrot)
2 medium onions, sliced
10 peppercorns

4 allspice
½ bay leaf
  dash of thyme
½ cup boiling vinegar
¾ cup butter, melted
  parsley
  lemon wedges

Carp is a traditional Christmas Eve dish.

Clean carp, cut lengthwise. Cook vegetables and spices in salted water for 20 minutes. Put carp in a large vessel, skin side up, and slowly pour vinegar over it. (Skin will turn blue.) Pour in vegetables with water, but not directly over the fish. Cover, and simmer for 15 to 20 minutes. Remove carp to a warm plate. Garnish with parsley and lemon wedges, and serve with butter. Serves 4 to 6.

BAKED FISH I
PEČENÉ RYBY

3 pounds fish
  salt to taste
¼ teaspoon caraway seeds

1 tablespoon lemon juice
⅔ cup butter

Split a large fish lengthwise, or use a small whole fish. Sprinkle with salt, caraway seeds, and lemon juice. Bake in butter in a 350° oven for 20 to 30 minutes. Serves 4 to 6.

BAKED FISH II
ZAPEČENÁ RYBA

1 pound fillets of sole or flounder	¼ cup shortening
1 tablespoon vinegar	½ cup milk
salt to taste	1 egg
	¼ cup flour

Sprinkle fillets with vinegar and salt. Place in a well-greased baking dish. Mix together well milk, egg, and flour; pour over fish. Bake in a 350° oven for 30 minutes. Serves 2.

BOILED FISH
VAŘENÁ RYBA

4 cups water	1 allspice
salt to taste	½ bay leaf
1 cup sliced vegetables (carrot, parsnip, celery root)	3 pounds fish (carp, pike, or trout)
1 medium onion, sliced	½ cup butter, melted
4 peppercorns	parsley
	lemon wedges

Cook vegetables and spices in salted water for 10 minutes. Add cleaned fish, cover, and steam for 15 to 25 minutes. Remove carefully, pour butter over. Serve garnished with parsley and lemon. Serves 4 to 6.

BROILED FISH
RYBY PEČENÉ NA ROŠTU

3 pounds fish	½ cup flour
salt to taste	½ cup melted butter or oil
2 tablespoons lemon juice or vinegar	

Leave small fish whole, but cut large fish into serving pieces. Sprinkle fish with salt and lemon juice or vinegar. Roll lightly in flour, and brush with butter. Broil 6 to 10 minutes, turning once and brushing with more butter. Serves 6.

MARINATED FISH
RYBY MARINOVANÉ

3 pounds fish (carp, pike,
    eel, trout, salmon,
    tuna, or mackerel)

salt to taste
¼ cup butter

MARINADE

1½ cups water
½ cup vinegar
¼ cup fish stock
2 medium onions, sliced
5 peppercorns
2 allspice

1 clove
½ bay leaf
1 large pickle, chopped
2 teaspoons chopped
    capers
¼ cup oil

Sprinkle fish with salt; bake in butter in a 350° oven for about 20 minutes. Boil together water, vinegar, stock, onion, and spices for 20 to 30 minutes; cool. Add pickle, capers, oil. Pour over fish; refrigerate for 24 hours. Serves 6.

FRIED FISH I
SMAŽENÉ RYBY OBALOVANÉ

3 pounds fish fillet
    salt to taste
½ cup flour
3 eggs, lightly beaten
1½ cups bread crumbs

¾–1 cup butter or lard
lemon wedges
horseradish
Tartar Sauce
    (see Index)
(optional)

Sprinkle fish with salt. Roll in flour, dip in egg, and roll in bread crumbs. Fry in butter, 7 to 10 minutes on each side. Serve with wedges of lemon, horseradish, or Tartar Sauce. Serves 6.

FRIED FISH II
SMAŽENÉ RYBY V TĚSTÍČKU

2 eggs
1 cup milk
1 cup flour
3 pounds fish fillets

salt to taste
¾ cup butter
lemon wedges

Mix together well eggs, milk, and flour. Sprinkle fish with salt, and dip in batter. Fry in hot butter, about 7 minutes on each side. Serve with lemon. Serves 6.

STEWED FISH IN WINE
RYBA NA VÍNĚ

6 tablespoons butter
1 onion, chopped
1 bay leaf
5 peppercorns
2 whole cloves
3 pounds fish (carp or
    pike)

salt to taste
1 cup red wine
½–1 cup water or fish
    stock
¼ cup flour
lemon juice to taste

Wilt onion in half the butter. Add bay leaf, peppercorns, cloves, and fish sprinkled with salt. Add wine, and simmer for about 15 minutes. Remove fish to a heated platter. Melt the remaining butter; blend in flour. Blend in wine sauce, and water or fish stock. Simmer for 5 minutes. Strain sauce over fish, and sprinkle with lemon juice. Serves 6 to 8.

FISH WITH ANCHOVIES
RYBA NA SARDELI

3 pounds fish
salt to taste
⅓ cup butter
2–3 anchovies, boned
and chopped
1 onion, chopped

1 tablespoon chopped
parsley
¼ cup flour
1 cup water or fish stock
1 cup sour cream

Cut cleaned fish into serving pieces; sprinkle with salt. Sauté in half the butter for 4 to 5 minutes on each side. Melt the remaining butter, add anchovies, onion, and parsley, and fry. Blend in flour, stir in water or fish stock, and simmer for 5 minutes. Strain. Add sour cream, blend well. Reheat sauce and pour over fish. Serves 6 to 8.

FISH WITH MUSTARD
RYBA NA HOŘČICI

2 pounds fish (in 1 piece)
salt to taste
4 teaspoons mustard
¼ cup butter
1 onion, chopped
2 tablespoons flour
lemon juice to taste
water

STOCK
2 cups water
1 cup diced soup greens
1 bay leaf
5 peppercorns
5 allspice

Cook ingredients for stock together for 20 minutes. Sprinkle fish with salt; spread mustard over it. Wilt onion in butter, add fish; brown. Add stock. Simmer for 15 minutes. Remove fish to a heated platter. Mix flour in enough water to make a paste, and blend into stock. Simmer again for 5 minutes. Add lemon juice to taste. Strain sauce over fish. Serves 4 to 5.

FISH LOAF
SEKANÁ Z RYB

2 pounds fish, boned and
ground
salt and pepper to taste
1 egg

1 clove garlic,
mashed
½ cup milk
1–1⅓ cups bread crumbs
¼ cup shortening,
melted

Mix together all ingredients except shortening; shape into 2 loaves. Place in a pan, brush generously with part of the shortening, and bake in the remaining shortening in a 350° oven for 30 minutes. Serves 4 to 6.

FISH PUDDING
RYBÍ PUDINK

2 pounds fish, boned
salt to taste
pepper to taste
2 hard rolls
2 eggs, lightly beaten

1 tablespoon grated
cheese
1 tablespoon flour
¼ cup butter, melted

Chop ¼ pound of the fish. Chop up the rolls and soak in water, then drain. Mix well with the chopped fish, seasonings, eggs, cheese, flour, and butter. Dice the remaining fish. Grease a pudding form and sprinkle with bread crumbs. Place a layer of fish filling in the form; cover with a layer of diced fish. Repeat the layering process, ending with a layer of filling. Steam for 1 hour (see Steamed Puddings for method). Serve with Tomato Sauce (see Index). Serves 6.

HERRING CASSEROLE
ZAPEČENÝ SLANEČEK

2 pounds potatoes, boiled,
   sliced
1 medium onion, chopped
½ cup butter

1 pound herring
2 cups milk
1 egg

Brown onion in 2 tablespoons butter; mix with potatoes. Soak herring in 1 cup milk; remove skin and bones, dice. Put half the potatoes in a greased pan, top with the herring, cover with the rest of the potatoes. Melt the remaining butter; pour over potatoes. Beat egg with 1 cup milk and pour over casserole. Bake in a 350° oven for 30 minutes. Serves 4 to 6.

SAUCES

WHITE SAUCE
ZAHUŠTĚNÁ OMÁČKA SVĚTLÁ

3 tablespoons butter
⅓ cup flour
2 cups stock

salt to taste
1 cup light cream or milk
1 or 2 egg yolks

Melt butter and blend in flour. Add stock and salt; simmer for 30 minutes. Mix cream with egg yolks and pour into sauce, stirring constantly. Do not boil. Serve over vegetables. Makes about 3 cups.

DILL SAUCE
KOPROVÁ OMÁČKA

Prepare White Sauce (above). Add 2 tablespoons minced dill. Add sugar and lemon juice to taste.

CHIVE SAUCE
PAŽITKOVÁ OMÁČKA

Prepare White Sauce (above). Add 1 tablespoon minced chives. Add lemon juice and sugar to taste.

LEMON SAUCE
CITRÓNOVÁ OMÁČKA

Prepare White Sauce (above). Add ½ teaspoon grated lemon peel, juice of 1 lemon, and 1 teaspoon sugar.

68

WHITE TOMATO SAUCE
RAJSKÁ OMÁČKA BÍLÁ

1 medium onion, chopped	1 cup water
2 tablespoons butter	¼ cup flour
½ pound tomatoes, diced	1 cup sour cream
salt to taste	

Wilt onion in butter; add tomatoes, salt, and water. Simmer for 10 minutes. Rub through a sieve, bring to a boil. Mix flour with sour cream; add to tomatoes. Bring to a boil. Makes about 3 cups.

WHITE ONION SAUCE
CIBULOVÁ OMÁČKA BÍLÁ

2 large onions, sliced	1 cup milk
2 tablespoons butter	salt to taste
1 cup boiling water	1 egg yolk
¼ cup flour	

Wilt onions in butter, pour in boiling water. Bring to a boil. Mix flour with milk and salt and pour into sauce. Simmer for 20 minutes. Rub through a sieve, then add egg yolk, mixed well in ¼ cup of cooled sauce. Do not boil. Makes about 2 cups.

SAUERBRATEN SAUCE
SVÍČKOVÁ OMÁČKA

1 carrot, chopped	2 cups stock
1 parsnip, chopped	4 peppercorns
½ celery root, chopped	2 allspice
1 medium onion, chopped	½ bay leaf
3 tablespoons butter	salt to taste
	vinegar to taste

Fry vegetables in butter. Add stock, peppercorns, allspice, bay leaf. Simmer for 30 minutes. Rub through a sieve. Add salt and vinegar.

LIVER SAUCE
JÁTROVÁ OMÁČKA

3 tablespoons lard	dash of marjoram
1 medium onion, chopped	2 cups vegetable stock
¼ pound liver, ground	¼ cup flour
¼ teaspoon caraway seeds	salt to taste
dash of pepper	

Brown onion in 1 tablespoon lard. Add liver and seasonings, and stir until brown. Pour in ½ cup stock; simmer for 8 minutes. Brown flour in 2 tablespoons lard, add remaining stock and salt; simmer for 30 minutes. Add liver mixture, and bring to a boil. Makes about 3 cups.

GOULASH SAUCE
GULÁŠOVÁ OMÁČKA

Prepare like Liver Sauce (above), but instead of liver, use diced beef or lamb, and add ¼ teaspoon paprika.

POLISH SAUCE
POLSKÁ OMÁČKA

1 medium onion, chopped	⅓ cup raisins
2 tablespoons butter	⅓ cup blanched almonds, sliced
¼ cup flour	2 teaspoons prune butter
1½ cups stock	2 teaspoons currant jam
¼ teaspoon grated lemon peel	salt to taste
	½ cup red wine

Fry onion in butter, add flour, and brown. Add stock, and simmer for 30 minutes. Strain. Add all other ingredients and simmer for 5 to 10 minutes.

This is very good with Boiled Beef or Boiled Beef Tongue (see Index).

PLAIN SAUCE
OMÁČKA ZAHUŠTĚNÁ JÍŠKOU

¼ cup flour   2 cups water or stock
2 tablespoons shortening   salt to taste

Fry flour in shortening until golden brown. Add liquid slowly, stirring constantly. Add salt, and simmer for 30 minutes. Makes about 2 cups.

GARLIC SAUCE
ČESNEKOVÁ OMÁČKA

Prepare Plain Sauce (above). Add 2 or 3 cloves of garlic, mashed, stirring well.

MARJORAM SAUCE
MAJORÁNKOVÁ OMÁČKA

Prepare Plain Sauce (above). Stir in ½ teaspoon marjoram.

CARAWAY SAUCE
KMÍNOVÁ OMÁČKA

Simmer ½ teaspoon caraway seeds with Plain Sauce (above). Add a dash of pepper, 1 teaspoon minced parsley, and a small clove of garlic, mashed, and stir in well.

MUSTARD SAUCE
HOŘČICOVÁ OMÁČKA

Prepare Plain Sauce (above). Add 1 small grated onion and 2 teaspoons prepared mustard. Simmer for 5 minutes.

CAPER SAUCE
KAPAROVÁ OMÁČKA

Prepare Plain Sauce (above). Add 1 tablespoon chopped capers and ¼ teaspoon grated lemon peel. Simmer for 5 minutes.

ANCHOVY SAUCE
SARDELOVÁ OMÁČKA

Prepare Plain Sauce (above). Fry 1 small onion, chopped, in 1 tablespoon butter. Add 2 mashed anchovies.

MUSHROOM SAUCE
HOUBOVÁ OMÁČKA

Prepare Plain Sauce (above). Fry 1 small onion, chopped, in 1 tablespoon butter. Add 2 cups sliced mushrooms and ¼ teaspoon caraway seeds; sauté for 20 to 30 minutes. Add to sauce. Before serving, add 2 teaspoons minced parsley.

ONION SAUCE
CIBULOVÁ OMÁČKA

Prepare Plain Sauce (above), but add 2 chopped onions to the shortening.

TOMATO SAUCE
RAJSKÁ OMÁČKA

1 recipe Plain Sauce (above)	2 allspice
1 small onion, chopped	½ bay leaf
1 cup tomatoes, chopped	dash of thyme
3 peppercorns	½ teaspoon sugar
	vinegar to taste

Simmer all ingredients but sugar and vinegar together for 30 minutes. Rub through a sieve. Add sugar and vinegar.

PICKLE SAUCE
OKURKOVÁ OMÁČKA

Prepare Plain Sauce (above). Add 2 large pickles, chopped, and ½ teaspoon sugar.

VEGETABLE SAUCE
ZELENINOVÁ OMÁČKA

½ pound vegetables, sliced (asparagus, celery, cauliflower, radish, leek)	2 cups water or stock
	⅓ cup flour
	salt to taste
	1 egg yolk
5 tablespoons butter	½ cup sour cream

Sauté vegetables (use either a single vegetable or a combination of two or more) in 2 tablespoons butter; add ½ cup water, and simmer until tender. In another pan, melt remaining butter, blend in flour, add the rest of the water. Simmer for 30 minutes. Add to vegetable mixture and simmer for 5 minutes. Blend egg yolk with sour cream; add to sauce, but do not boil. Makes about 3 cups.

BUTTER TO SERVE WITH FISH
MÁSLO K RYBĚ

½ pound butter	1 tablespoon minced parsley
salt to taste	
lemon juice to taste	

Melt butter. Add all ingredients.

HORSERADISH WITH APPLES
JABLEČNÝ KŘEN

2 tablespoons grated horseradish	2 apples, peeled and grated salt to taste
2 tablespoons cold stock	lemon juice to taste

Mix together all ingredients. Serve with boiled meat.

CREAM SAUCE
SMETANOVÁ OMÁČKA

2 cups light cream	salt to taste
¼ cup flour	2 tablespoons chopped
½ cup milk	blanched almonds

Bring cream to a boil. Pour in milk mixed with flour. Stir constantly. Simmer over low heat for 15 minutes. Add salt and almonds.

HORSERADISH SAUCE
KŘENOVÁ OMÁČKA

Prepare Cream Sauce (above). Add 2 tablespoons grated horseradish.

VEGETABLE CREAM SAUCE
ZELENINOVÁ OMÁČKA

Prepare Cream Sauce (above). Add 1 tablespoon cooked diced carrot, 1 tablespoon cooked diced celery root, 1 table-spoon cooked diced cauliflower, and 1 tablespoon cooked green peas.

DILL CREAM SAUCE
KOPROVÁ OMÁČKA

Prepare Cream Sauce (above). Add 1 tablespoon chopped dill, 1 egg yolk, vinegar and sugar to taste.

CHIVE SAUCE
PAŽITKOVÁ OMÁČKA

Prepare Cream Sauce (above). Add 1 tablespoon chopped chives, 1 egg yolk, vinegar and sugar to taste.

MUSHROOM CREAM SAUCE
HOUBOVÁ OMÁČKA

2 cups sliced mushrooms	pinch of caraway seeds
¾ cup water	¼ cup flour
salt to taste	1 cup sour cream

Simmer mushrooms in salted water with caraway seeds until tender (20 to 30 minutes). Mix sour cream with flour; add, stirring constantly. Simmer for 5 minutes. Makes about 3 cups.

HORSERADISH WITH BREAD CRUMBS
HOUSKOVÝ KŘEN

2 tablespoons grated horseradish	salt to taste
¼ cup bread crumbs	sugar to taste
½ cup hot stock	vinegar to taste

Mix together all ingredients. Serve with boiled beef or pork.

HOMEMADE MAYONNAISE
MAJONÉZA

2 egg yolks
    salt to taste

1 cup oil
1 tablespoon lemon juice

Beat egg yolks well with salt until creamy. Add oil, drop by drop, stirring vigorously all the while. Add lemon juice; blend well. (If mayonnaise curdles, correct as follows: Put 1 egg yolk into a clean bowl, add salt, beat until creamy. Add curdled mayonnaise by spoonfuls, stirring constantly.) Makes 1½ cups mayonnaise.

TARTAR SAUCE
TATARSKÁ OMÁČKA

1 recipe Homemade
    Mayonnaise (above)
1 teaspoon minced parsley
1 teaspoon chopped
    pickle
½ small onion, chopped

¼ teaspoon grated lemon
    peel
1 teaspoon chopped
    capers
1 anchovy, mashed

Blend all ingredients together well.

CAVIAR SAUCE
KAVIÁROVÁ OMÁČKA

Mix 1 tablespoon caviar into 1 recipe Homemade Mayonnaise (above).

HORSERADISH WITH CREAM
SMETANOVÝ KŘEN

2 tablespoons grated
    horseradish
2 tablespoons light cream
    salt to taste

1 teaspoon sugar
1 cup Whipped Cream
    (see Index)

Blend together all ingredients. Fold in whipped cream. Serve with fish or game.

CARROT HORSERADISH
MRKVOVÝ KŘEN

1¼ cups grated carrot	2 tablespoons vinegar
¼ cup grated horseradish	salt to taste
⅓ cup water	sugar to taste

Blend together all ingredients. Serve with boiled meat, cold roast, hamburgers, etc.

HOLLANDAISE SAUCE
HOLANDSKÁ OMÁČKA JEMNÁ

6 egg yolks	salt to taste
1 cup water or stock	lemon juice to taste
¾ cup butter	

Put egg yolks into a double boiler, blend with water, butter, salt, and lemon juice. Heat slowly until sauce thickens, stirring constantly. Do not boil. Makes about 2 cups.

THRIFTY HOLLANDAISE SAUCE
HOLANDSKÁ LEVNÁ

1 teaspoon cornstarch	½ cup butter
1 cup water or stock	salt to taste
3 egg yolks	lemon juice to taste

Mix cornstarch with liquid, blend in all other ingredients gradually, and heat slowly in a double boiler until sauce thickens, stirring constantly. Do not boil. Serve with fish or vegetables.

EGGS, CHEESE AND NOODLE DISHES

BAKED EGGS WITH CHICKEN LIVERS
VEJCE V KELÍMCÍCH S KUŘECÍMI JÁTRY

4 chicken livers, chopped
¼ cup butter
  salt to taste
  pepper to taste
4 tablespoons cooked
  green peas

4–8 eggs
1 teaspoon minced
  parsley
2 teaspoons grated
  cheese

Brown chicken livers in half the butter. Divide into 4 greased custard cups; sprinkle with salt. Place 1 tablespoon peas in each cup, and break in 1 or 2 eggs. Sprinkle with salt and pepper. Top with remaining butter; sprinkle with parsley and cheese. Place cups in a pan of boiling water and bake in a preheated 350° oven until eggs are set (about 20 minutes). Serves 4.

EGGS SURPRISE
OBALOVANÁ VEJCE

4 hard-cooked eggs,
  shelled
4 slices ham or bologna
4 thin slices veal cutlets
  salt to taste

¼ cup flour
1 egg, lightly beaten
½ cup bread crumbs
  shortening for frying

Wrap each hard-cooked egg in a slice of ham or bologna, then in veal. Sprinkle with salt. Roll in flour, dip in egg, and roll in bread crumbs. Fry to a golden brown.

Serve hot with mashed potatoes, or serve cold, cut in half lengthwise, with potato salad. Serves 2 to 4.

EGG TOADSTOOLS
MUCHOMURKY

6 hard-cooked eggs
3 anchovies
¾ cup (approximately) butter

3 tomatoes
2 cups finely chopped lettuce

Peel eggs. Slice a piece off the wider end of each so the yolk can be removed with a small spoon. Mash anchovies with butter and egg yolks; stuff mixture into hollowed egg whites. Arrange lettuce on a serving dish; stand the eggs, cut side down, on it. Cut tomatoes into halves, and place a half on each egg as a "cap." Dot with additional creamed butter. Serves 6.

CHEESE OMELET
TVAROHOVÝ TRHANEC

3 tablespoons butter
¼ cup sugar
4 eggs, separated
2 cups farmer cheese

½ cup milk
1 cup flour
¼ cup butter for pan

Cream butter, sugar, and egg yolks until foamy. Rub cheese through strainer, add to butter mixture. Mix in milk and flour. Fold in stiffly beaten egg whites. Melt the ¼ cup butter in a baking pan, pour in batter. Bake in a preheated 300° oven for 15 to 20 minutes. Tear into small pieces, turn over, and bake 10 minutes longer. Sprinkle with sugar. Serve with a fruit sirup. Serves 4.

CZECH OMELET
TRHANEC

4 eggs, separated	2¼ cups flour
¼ cup sugar	4 tablespoons butter for
dash of salt	pan
2 cups milk	

Beat together egg yolks, sugar, salt, and half the milk. Add flour and the remaining milk. Beat until smooth. Fold in stiffly beaten egg whites. Melt 1 tablespoon butter in a pan, pour in one-quarter of the batter. Fry on both sides until golden brown. Tear with two forks into bite-size pieces; sprinkle with sugar. Serve with fruit sirup. Repeat to make three more omelets. Serves 4.

FARINA OMELET
KRUPICOVY TRHANEC

4 eggs, separated	1 cup farina
¼ cup sugar	¼ cup butter for pan
dash of salt	2 cups milk

Beat egg yolks, sugar, salt and farina with half the milk. Let stand for 1 hour. Blend in remaining milk; fold in stiffly beaten egg whites. Melt butter in a baking pan, pour in batter. Bake in a preheated 300° oven for 30 minutes. Tear into small pieces, turn over, and bake 20 minutes longer. Sprinkle with sugar and serve with fruit sirup or Stewed Fruit (see Index). Serves 4.

PUFFY OMELET
SVÍTEK

3–4 eggs, separated	2–2¼ cups flour
3 tablespoons sugar	pinch of baking
dash of salt	powder
2 cups milk	¼ cup butter for pan

Beat egg yolks with sugar, salt, and half the milk. Sift flour with baking powder; add to egg mixture alternately with the remaining milk, a little at a time. Beat into a thick batter. Fold in stiffly beaten egg whites. Melt butter in a baking pan, pour in batter. Bake in a preheated 375° oven for 10 to 15 minutes, or until bottom is browned. Cut in four pieces, turn over, and brown the other side (cook 10 to 15 minutes longer). Sprinkle with sugar. Serve with a fruit sirup or Stewed Fruit (see Index). Serves 4.

PUFFY OMELET WITH CRANBERRIES
SVÍTEK S BRUSINKAMI

OMELET

1 large egg
½ cup flour
½ cup milk
  dash of salt
1 teaspoon sugar
2 tablespoons butter

FILLING

1 cup fresh cranberries
⅓ cup sugar

Beat together all ingredients for omelet except butter until smooth. Melt butter in a frying pan, pour in batter. Bake in a preheated 400° oven 15 to 20 minutes. The omelet should puff up at the sides and be crisp. If the center should pucker, prick with a fork. Fill with cranberries and serve at once.

To prepare filling, wash cranberries, and without drying them, place in a pot. Cook over low heat for 2 or 3 minutes. Add sugar; simmer for 10 minutes. Serves 1 or 2.

OMELETS
OMELETY

3–5 eggs, separated
    pinch of salt
¼ cup sugar

2 cups milk
1⅓ cups flour
⅓ cup shortening for pan
jam

Beat egg yolks, salt, sugar, and half the milk. Add flour, and beat until smooth. Mix in the remaining milk, a little at a time. Fold in stiffly beaten egg whites. Fry omelets in a greased pan to ⅛- or ³⁄₁₆-inch thickness. Fill each with jam; fold over. Serves 3 to 5.

SIDE DISH OMELETS
SLANÉ OMELETY

Prepare like Omelets (above), but omit sugar, and add salt to taste. Before cooking, blend in ½ cup grated cheese or ½ to 1 cup cooked and chopped vegetable or meat. Serve with meat, vegetables, or green salad. Serves 3 to 5.

OMELETS WITH CHEESE FILLING
OMELETY S TVAROHEM

1 recipe Omelets (see
    Index)
1 recipe Cheese Filling
    (see Index)

½ cup milk
1 tablespoon sugar
1 egg

Make omelets thin. Spread cheese filling on top, and roll up. Place in greased baking dish. Beat milk, sugar, and egg, and pour over omelets. Bake in a preheated 350° oven for about 30 minutes or until all the liquid is absorbed. Serves 4 to 6.

OMELETS WITH APPLE FILLING
OMELETY S JABLKOVOU NÁDIVKOU

1 recipe Omelets (see Index)	⅓ cup almonds, blanched and sliced
2 eggs, separated	1 tablespoon butter, melted
⅓ cup sugar	
2 cups applesauce	

Make omelets thick. Cream egg yolks with sugar. Add applesauce and almonds. Fold in stiffly beaten egg whites. Grease a spring form and sprinkle with fine bread crumbs. Put in one omelet, spread with apple filling. Repeat; top all with omelet. Sprinkle with melted butter. Bake in a preheated 350° oven for about 30 minutes. Remove from form, sprinkle with sugar. Serve the omelets cut into wedges. Serves 6.

POTATO OMELETS
BRAMBOROVÝ TRHANEC

1 cup grated boiled potatoes	1 cup milk
¼ cup sugar dash of salt	2 cups flour
2 eggs	¼ cup butter for pan, melted

Mix all ingredients to a smooth batter. Brush a frying pan with butter; fry omelets to a golden brown. Tear into small pieces, and sprinkle with sugar. Serves 4.

CHEESE SOUFFLÉ
TVAROHOVÝ NÁKYP

6 tablespoons butter
¾ cup sugar
3 eggs, separated

1⅔ cups farmer cheese,
   rubbed through a
   sieve
¼ cup farina
   instantized flour

Cream butter with sugar and egg yolks until foamy. Add cheese and farina. Fold in stiffly beaten egg whites. Grease a soufflé dish and sprinkle with instantized flour. Pour in mixture and bake in a preheated 350° oven for 45 minutes. Serve with fruit sirup. Serves 4.

FARINA SOUFFLÉ
KRUPICOVÝ NÁKYP

2 cups milk
   dash of salt
½ cup plus 1 tablespoon
   farina
¼ cup butter

½ cup superfine sugar
3 eggs, separated
½ teaspoon grated lemon
   peel

Bring milk and salt to a boil. Add farina, and cook 8 to 10 minutes, stirring constantly. Cool. Cream butter with sugar and egg yolks until foamy. Add farina mixture by spoonfuls, then add lemon peel. Beat egg whites until stiff, stir two spoonfuls into farina mixture; fold in the remaining whites. Pour into a greased soufflé dish sprinkled with bread crumbs, and bake in a preheated 350° oven for 45 minutes. Serve with fruit sirup or Caramel Sauce (see Index). Serves 4.

NOODLE SOUFFLÉ
NUDLOVÝ NÁKYP

2⅔ cups milk
dash of salt
½ pound wide egg
noodles
5 tablespoons butter

5 tablespoons sugar
3 eggs, separated
1 teaspoon vanilla
1 pound apples, peeled,
cored, and sliced

Bring milk and salt to a boil. Add noodles. Cook until thick, stirring constantly. Cool. Cream butter with sugar, add egg yolks, and beat until foamy. Add cooked noodles and vanilla. Fold in stiffly beaten egg whites. Pour half the mixture into a greased baking dish, arrange apples on top, then pour in the remaining mixture. Bake in a preheated 350° oven 30 to 45 minutes. Sprinkle with sugar. Serves 4 to 6.

NOODLE SOUFFLÉ WITH CHERRIES
AND NUTS
NUDLOVÝ NÁKYP TŘEŠŇOVÝ S OŘÍŠKY

1 recipe Noodle Soufflé
⅓ cup ground nuts

1 pound cherries, pitted

Prepare Noodle Soufflé mixture, but use cherries in place of apples. Fold nuts into batter before layering in baking dish. Serves 4 to 6.

RICE SOUFFLÉ
RÝŽOVÝ NÁKYP

3 cups milk	1 teaspoon grated lemon
½ cup butter	peel
½ cup plus 2 tablespoons	1 teaspoon vanilla
sugar	⅓ cup grated nuts
1 cup rice	3 apples, peeled, cored,
3 eggs, separated	and sliced

Bring milk to a boil. Add ¼ cup of the butter, ¼ cup of the sugar, and rice. Cook until rice is done (about 14 minutes). Cool. Cream remaining butter and sugar, add egg yolks, beat until foamy. Add lemon peel, vanilla, nuts, and the cooked rice. Fold in stiffly beaten egg whites. Pour half the mixture into a greased soufflé dish. Arrange apples on top. Pour the remaining mixture over all. Bake in a preheated 350° oven for about 1 hour. Serves 4 to 6.

HARD ROLL SOUFFLÉ
ŽEMLOVÝ NÁKYP

6 hard rolls, sliced	½ teaspoon grated lemon
2 cups hot milk	peel
¼ cup butter	3 apricot kernels, grated
½ cup plus 2 tablespoons	1 tablespoon farina
sugar	1 tablespoon cocoa
3 eggs, separated	

Pour milk over rolls; cool. Rub through a strainer. Cream butter with sugar and egg yolks until foamy. Add lemon peel, apricot kernels, and rolls. Fold in stiffly beaten egg whites and farina mixed with the cocoa. Grease a baking dish, and sprinkle with fine bread crumbs. Pour in the mixture, and bake in a preheated 350° oven for 35 to 45 minutes. Serve with Stewed Fruit (see Index) or a fruit sirup. Serves 4 to 6.

COOKED CHEESE
SÝR VAŘENÝ

1 pound farmer cheese
1 teaspoon salt
1 teaspoon caraway seeds

1 teaspoon paprika
1 cup butter
2 egg yolks, lightly beaten

Place cheese in layers in a china bowl, sprinkling each layer with salt, caraway seeds, and paprika. Cover and let stand in a cool place (not a refrigerator) for three days. The cheese should be slightly runny. Melt butter, add cheese to it. Heat, stirring constantly, until cheese is melted and creamy. Add egg yolks and mix well. Pour into a bowl or a mold, and chill. Slice to serve.

FRIED CHEESE
SÝR SMAŽENÝ

4 slices Swiss or Gouda
       cheese cut ¾ to 1
       inch thick
    salt to taste

½ cup flour
1 egg, beaten
⅔ cup bread crumbs
1 cup shortening

Sprinkle cheese with salt. Dip slices first in flour, then in beaten egg; roll in bread crumbs. Fry quickly in hot shortening until golden brown. Serve with mashed potatoes or vegetables. Serves 2.

CHEESE PUDDING
SÝROVÝ PUDINK

1⅔ cups flour
  1 cup sour cream or milk
  4 eggs, separated

1 cup grated cheese
salt to taste

Mix flour with cream and egg yolks. Add cheese and salt. Fold in stiffly beaten egg whites. Steam for 30 minutes (see Steamed Puddings for method). Serves 6.

NOODLES
NUDLE

3 cups instantized flour
2 eggs, lightly beaten
½ cup water

Mix eggs and water. Heap flour on a pastry board and make a well in the center. Pour egg mixture into the well. Mix with a fork at first, then knead into an elastic shiny dough. Cut into 3 pieces, cover with a napkin, and let stand for 30 minutes. Roll each piece out as thin as possible without tearing. Let dry for a few minutes. Cut into strips about 2 to 3 inches wide, or roll up and slice for longer noodles. Cut into desired width (⅛ inch for soup, ¾ inch for wide noodles). Cook in 4 quarts of salted boiling water for 4 to 5 minutes, stirring often. Drain. Serves 3 to 4.

NOODLE AND HAM CASSEROLE
FLÍČKY SE ŠUNKOU

1 recipe Noodles (see
  above)
¼ cup butter, melted
1 pound ham or smoked
  meat, diced

3 eggs, lightly beaten
1 cup milk
salt to taste

Prepare noodle dough and cut into ¾-inch squares. Cook in salted boiling water for 4 to 5 minutes. Drain. Mix with butter and ham. Put into a well-greased casserole. Mix the eggs, milk, and salt, and pour over noodles. Bake in a 350° oven for 30 to 45 minutes, or until eggs are set. Serves 4.

NOODLES WITH FARMER CHEESE
NUDLE S TVAROHEM

1 recipe Noodles (see
  Index)
½ cup butter, melted

1 cup farmer cheese
⅓ cup sugar

Prepare noodles. Mix half the butter with cooked, drained noodles. Arrange on a plate, sprinkle with crumbled cheese, sugar, and the remaining butter. Serves 3 to 4.

NOODLES WITH POPPY SEEDS OR GINGERBREAD
NUDLE S MÁKEM NEBO PERNÍKEM

1 recipe Noodles (see Index)
½ cup butter, melted

½–¾ cup ground poppy seeds or grated gingerbread
⅓ cup sugar

Prepare noodles. Mix half the butter with cooked, drained noodles. Arrange on a plate. Mix poppy seeds or gingerbread with sugar, and sprinkle over the noodles. Pour the remaining butter over all. Serves 3 to 4.

NOODLES WITH MUSHROOMS
NUDLE S HOUBAMI

1 recipe Noodles (see Index)

1 recipe Sautéed Mushrooms (see Index)

Prepare wide noodles. Mix cooked noodles with sautéed mushrooms. Heat thoroughly. Serves 3 to 4.

NOODLES WITH SPINACH
NUDLE SE ŠPENÁTEM

1 recipe Noodles (see Index)
1 small onion, chopped
¼ cup butter

1 pound spinach, cleaned, cooked, and chopped
salt to taste

Prepare noodles. Wilt onion in butter, add spinach and salt. Sauté for 5 minutes, add cooked noodles. Mix. Serves 3 to 4.

DUMPLINGS AND PANCAKES

RAISED DUMPLINGS
KYNUTÉ KNEDLÍKY

¾ teaspoon compressed
    yeast (see Explana-
    tory Notes)
1 cup warm milk
1 egg
1 teaspoon salt

4 cups instantized
    flour
1–1½ pounds fruit
    (cherries, straw-
    berries, blue-
    berries, etc.)

Dissolve yeast in ¼ cup of the milk, and let stand in a warm place until bubbly. Mix together remaining milk, egg, and salt, and pour into flour. Add yeast, and beat into a firm dough. Dust top with flour, cover with a clean napkin, and let rise in a warm place until double in bulk (about 1 hour). Punch down. Break into pieces big enough to wrap fruit (dough casing should be about ¼ inch thick). Pinch dough edges together, sealing well so fruit juices cannot escape. Lay dumplings on a floured board, cover with a napkin, and let rise about 15 to 20 minutes. Cook in a tightly covered pot in boiling salted water for 5 minutes. Uncover, turn dumplings over, and cook 3 to 5 minutes longer (depending on size). Remove from pot with a skimmer, and immediately tear open with 2 forks. Serve with melted butter and sugar, ground poppy seeds, grated gingerbread, or farmer cheese.

These dumplings may be made with almost any kind of fruit, but are best filled with soft fruit or jams or preserves. They may also be cooked without any filling, and served with meat. Serves 4 to 6.

FARINA DUMPLINGS I
KRUPICOVÉ NOČKY

½ cup milk
  salt to taste
¼ cup farina

2 tablespoons butter
1 egg
dash of mace

Bring milk, salt, and farina to a slow boil, stir until thick. Cool. Add butter, egg, and mace. Drop in small amounts from a wet spoon into boiling soup; simmer for 3 to 5 minutes.

FARINA DUMPLINGS II
KRUPICOVÉ NOKY

1½ cups milk
  1 teaspoon salt
  ⅓ cup butter

1½ cups farina
3–4 eggs

Scald milk with salt and butter. Add farina, stirring constantly. Cook until dough does not stick to spoon. Add eggs, 1 at a time, beating well. Drop batter by small spoonfuls into boiling water and cook for 4 or 5 minutes. Serve with creamed dishes or bread crumbs fried in butter, and a salad. Or serve as a dessert, with Stewed Fruit (see Index) or a sweet sauce. Serves 4 to 6.

LARGE FARINA DUMPLING
KRUPICOVÝ KNEDLÍK

1¼ cups farina
  1 cup milk
  1 teaspoon salt

2 eggs, lightly beaten
2 cups diced stale white
  bread

Pour farina and salt into scalded milk. Let stand for 30 minutes. Add eggs; mix well. Mix in bread. Cook like Napkin Dumpling I (see Index) for 45 minutes. Serves 4.

NAPKIN DUMPLING I
TŘENÝ KNEDLÍK

⅔ cup butter
4 eggs, separated
1 teaspoon salt
¾ cup milk

4 cups instantized flour
4 cups diced stale white
    bread
2 tablespoons butter

Cream ⅔ cup butter. Add egg yolks, 1 at a time, mixing well. Dissolve salt in milk and add liquid, alternately with flour, by spoonfuls to butter-egg mixture. Add the bread cubes, which have been fried in the 2 tablespoons butter, and mix in well. Fold in stiffly beaten egg whites.

Wet a large napkin; wring out. Place in a sieve; pour in dough. Pull napkin up around dough and tie in 2 places with a thread: first right above mound of dough, then ¾ inch above that. Tie napkin corners over a wooden spoon and place this across a deep pot containing boiling water. Dumpling must be completely submerged but must not touch the bottom of the pot, and it should hang about 2 inches below water surface. Cook for 20 minutes, then untie the first thread. Continue to cook 40 minutes longer. Remove dumpling from napkin, and slice with thread. Slide a piece of thread about 20 inches long under dumpling; to slice dumpling, switch ends from one hand to the other, and pull. Serves 6 to 8.

NAPKIN DUMPLING II
JEMNÝ HOUSKOVÝ KNEDLÍK

4 cups instantized flour
2 cups milk
1 teaspoon salt
4 eggs, separated

4 cups diced stale white
    bread
⅓ cup butter, melted

Sift flour into a bowl. In another bowl, mix milk, salt, and egg yolks well; pour into flour. Work with a wooden spoon until dough is shiny; sprinkle with bread, then with butter.

Let stand for 1 hour, then mix well and fold in stiffly beaten egg whites. Cook like Napkin Dumpling I (above). Serves 6 to 8.

FLOUR DUMPLINGS
MOUČNÉ NOKY

¼ cup butter
1 teaspoon salt
1 egg

¼ teaspoon single-acting baking powder (see Explanatory Notes)
4 cups flour
1½ cups milk

Cream butter with salt. Add egg, and beat until foamy. Sift baking powder with flour; add by spoonfuls, alternately with milk, to butter mixture. Let stand for 30 minutes. Drop by spoonfuls into boiling water and cook for 8 to 10 minutes. Serves 4 to 6.

FARINA FRUIT DUMPLINGS
TĚSTO Z KRUPICOVÉ KAŠE

1½ cups milk
¾ cup farina
¼ teaspoon salt
1 egg
1 tablespoon sugar

1–1½ cups (approximately) instantized flour
1–1½ pounds fruit

Cook milk and farina for 5 minutes to make a porridge. Cool. Add salt, egg, sugar, and enough flour to make a firm dough. Break off pieces and wrap around fruit (dough casing should be about ⅛ inch thick), sealing well so fruit juices cannot escape. Drop into boiling water and cook for 5 to 7 minutes, turning once. Remove with a skimmer and tear open with 2 forks. Serve with melted butter and sugar, ground poppy seeds, stale grated gingerbread, or cottage cheese. Serves 4 to 6.

SCALDED DOUGH DUMPLINGS I
TĚSTO SPAŘENÉ

2 cups instantized flour
1 teaspoon salt
1 cup milk
¼ cup butter, melted

1 whole egg
1 egg yolk
1–1½ pounds fruit

Sift flour and salt into a bowl. Scald milk with butter, and pour over flour. Mix well. Cool. Blend in egg and yolk. Shape dumplings and cook them like Farina Fruit Dumplings (see Index). Serves 4 to 6.

SCALDED DOUGH DUMPLINGS II
TĚSTO PÁLENÉ

1 cup milk
¼ cup butter
2 cups instantized flour

1 teaspoon salt
3 egg yolks
1–1½ pounds fruit

Bring milk and butter to a boil. Pour in flour all at once and beat quickly. When a ball forms, remove pot from heat. Add salt and egg yolks, one at a time, mixing well. Shape and cook dumplings like Farina Fruit Dumplings (see Index). Serves 4 to 6.

CHEESE FRUIT DUMPLINGS
TĚSTO TVAROHOVÉ

2 tablespoons butter
1 egg
½ cup pot cheese
 dash of salt
2 cups instantized flour

½ cup milk
1–1½ pounds fruit (fresh prunes, apricots, cherries, apples, or any other firm fruit)

Cream butter, egg, and cheese together thoroughly. Add salt, flour, and milk to make a medium-firm dough. Break off pieces and wrap around fruit (dough should be ³⁄₁₆ inch thick), sealing edges well. Cook in boiling water for 5 to 8 minutes, turning once. When dumplings are done, remove with a skimmer and tear open with 2 forks. Serve with melted butter, more cheese, and sugar. Serves 4 to 6.

WHITE BREAD DUMPLINGS I
HOUSKOVÝ KNEDLÍK

4 cups instantized flour	1½ cups milk
1 teaspoon salt	4 cups diced stale white
2 egg yolks	bread

Sift flour into a bowl. In another bowl, lightly beat together salt, egg yolks, and milk, and pour into flour. Work dough until it is shiny and does not stick to bowl; cover, and let stand for 1 hour. Work in the bread. With floured hands, shape dough into 3 or 4 rolls, 8 by 2½ inches. Bring about 6 quarts of water to a boil in a large pan and put in dumplings, making sure they do not stick to bottom. Cover, and cook for 10 to 15 minutes on each side (20 to 30 minutes in all). Remove from pan with 2 plates or a large skimmer. Make a cut across the center of 1 dumpling to make sure it is done, then slice all into ¾-inch pieces with a thin sharp knife or a thread. Arrange slices in a heated bowl. Serves 6 to 8.

WHITE BREAD DUMPLINGS II
HOUSKOVÝ KNEDLÍK S PRÁŠKEM

4 cups instantized flour	1 egg yolk
¼ teaspoon single-acting	1½ cups milk
baking powder (see	4 cups diced stale white
Explanatory Notes)	bread
1 teaspoon salt	

Sift flour and baking powder into a bowl, then proceed as for White Bread Dumplings I (above). Serves 6 to 8.

WHITE BREAD DUMPLINGS III
HOUSKOVÝ KNEDLÍK S DROŽDÍM

4 cups instantized flour
½ teaspoon compressed
　　yeast (see Explana-
　　tory Notes)
1 teaspoon salt

1 egg yolk
1–1½ cups milk
4 cups diced stale
　　white bread

Sift flour into a bowl, sprinkle crumbled yeast over it, then proceed as for White Bread Dumplings I (above). Serves 6 to 8.

WHITE BREAD DUMPLINGS IV
KNEDLÍK Z KRÁJENÝCH ŽEMLÍ

11 cups (1 pound and 1
　　cup) diced stale
　　white bread
1½ cups milk
3–4 eggs, lightly beaten

1 teaspoon salt
½ cup butter or bacon fat,
　　melted and cooled
⅓ cup instantized flour

Put bread into a large bowl. Mix milk, eggs, and salt, and pour over bread. Add butter or fat. Let mixture stand for 1 hour, or until all the liquid is absorbed, turning over gently a few times. Add flour and mix well. Turn out on a floured pastry board. To make dumplings, pinch off pieces of dough the size of oranges. Cook in salted boiling water for 20 to 25 minutes. Remove dumplings from water with a skimmer, and immediately tear open with 2 forks.

This dough may also be cooked as one large Napkin Dumpling (see Index). Serves 6.

DUMPLINGS WITH SMOKED MEAT
KNEDLÍKY S UZENYM MASEM

11 cups (1 pound and 1
    cup) diced stale
    white bread
2 cups milk
3 eggs, lightly beaten
1 teaspoon salt

¼ cup instantized flour
1–2 cups diced cooked
    smoked meat or
    ham
½ cup bacon fat, melted

Put bread into a large bowl. Mix together milk, eggs, and salt; pour over bread. Let stand for 1 hour, turning over gently a few times. Add flour and mix well. Add meat and cooled bacon fat; mix well. Shape and cook like White Bread Dumplings IV (see Index). Serve with more melted bacon fat and fried bread crumbs, or sauerkraut. Serves 6 to 8.

POTATO DUMPLINGS I (COLD POTATOES)
BRAMBOROVÉ KNEDLÍKY ZE
STUDENÝCH BRAMBOR

2 pounds potatoes
    salt to taste
3¼ cups instantized flour

2 eggs
    boiling salted water

Boil potatoes, let stand until the next day. Peel and grate. Add salt, flour, and eggs. Knead into firm dough. Do not let dough stand too long because it will get thin. Form into 4 rolls about 2½ inches in diameter. Boil in water for 15 to 20 minutes. Make sure dumplings do not stick to the bottom of the pan. Remove from water and slice. Serves 4 to 6.

POTATO DUMPLINGS II (RAW POTATOES)
CHLUPATÉ KNEDLÍKY

2 pounds potatoes, peeled	3 cups instantized flour
salt to taste	¼ cup lard, melted
1 egg	

Grate raw potatoes; drain. Add salt, egg, and flour. Mix well. Drop by spoonfuls into boiling salted water, and cook 6 to 8 minutes. Make sure dumplings do not stick to the bottom of the pan. Remove with a skimmer. Pour lard over dumplings, and serve with browned onion or sauerkraut. Serves 4 to 6.

POTATO DUMPLINGS III (HOT POTATOES)
BRAMBOROVÉ KNEDLÍKY Z
HORKÝCH BRAMBOR

2 pounds potatoes, peeled	¼ teaspoon single-acting baking powder (see Explanatory Notes)
salt to taste	
¾ cup farina	
1 egg	
2–2¼ cups instantized flour	2 cups croutons
	½ cup butter, melted

Boil potatoes; drain. Quickly add salt and farina, and mash smooth. Add egg and flour mixed with baking powder, and knead well. Knead in croutons. Form into balls about 3 inches in diameter. Boil in salted water for 15 minutes. Remove with a skimmer and immediately tear open with 2 forks. Serve with butter. Serves 4 to 6.

FILLED POTATO DUMPLINGS
PLNĚNÉ BRAMBOROVÉ KNEDLÍKY

Prepare dough for Potato Dumplings II (see Index), but omit croutons. Roll into 3-inch rectangles ¾ inch thick. Place 2 tablespoons diced cooked smoked meat in each center, seal, and roll into balls. Boil in salted water 8 to 10 minutes. Serves 4 to 6.

PLAIN PANCAKES
LÍVANCE

1 tablespoon compressed yeast (see Explanatory Notes)	½ teaspoon grated lemon peel
2 tablespoons sugar	⅓ cup butter (for pan)
2½–2¾ cups flour	½ cup jam (optional)
2 cups (approximately) milk	cinnamon sugar (½ cup sugar mixed with 1 teaspoon cinnamon—optional)
1 egg or 2 egg yolks	
pinch of salt	

Stir yeast and sugar together until mixture liquifies, and to it add 1 tablespoon flour and 1 or 2 tablespoons lukewarm milk. Let rise for 5 to 10 minutes (until mixture is bubbly). Add eggs, salt, and lemon peel; beat until well blended. Add flour and milk, and mix until batter is smooth. Let rise in a warm place for about 30 minutes or until doubled in bulk. Heat a heavy frying pan or griddle and brush with butter. Spoon in batter. Make pancakes about 4 inches across; turn to brown on both sides. Spread with jam, or dip in cinnamon sugar. Serves 4.

SOUR CREAM PANCAKES
LÍVANEČKY Z KYSELÉ SMETANY

2 egg yolks
¼ cup sugar
1 cup sour cream
dash of salt
1–1¼ cups flour

pinch of single-acting
baking powder (see
Explanatory Notes)
4 egg whites, beaten
stiffly
¼ cup butter

Beat egg yolks with sugar, sour cream, and salt. Mix in flour sifted with baking powder. Fold in egg whites. Heat a hèavy frying pan or griddle and brush with butter. Spoon in batter. Make pancakes small (3 inches), and turn to brown on both sides. Sprinkle with sugar. Serves 2 to 4.

THIN PANCAKES
PALAČINKY

2 eggs
pinch of salt
3 tablespoons sugar
2 cups milk

2 cups flour
¼ cup butter for pan
jam

Beat together eggs, salt, sugar, milk, and flour until smooth. Heat a frying pan; brush with butter. Pour in a thin layer of batter, and spread by tilting the pan. Pancakes must be very thin—almost transparent. Fry on both sides to a golden brown. Spread with jam, roll up, and keep warm until served. Dust with sugar. Serves 4 to 6.

VEGETABLES

BAKED ASPARAGUS
CHŘEST ZAPÉKANÝ

3 tablespoons flour
¼ cup butter
1 cup milk or water
   salt to taste

dash of nutmeg
1 pound asparagus, boiled
⅓ cup grated cheese

Brown flour in half the butter. Add milk, salt, and nutmeg. Simmer sauce for 5 minutes. Arrange asparagus in a greased casserole in layers with sauce, and sprinkle with cheese. Dot with the remaining butter and bake in 350° oven for 30 minutes. Serves 2.

CREAMED ASPARAGUS
CHŘEST DUŠENÝ

1 pound asparagus, cut
   into 2-inch pieces
1⅓ cups water
   salt to taste
2 tablespoons flour

2 tablespoons butter
½ cup cream
1 egg yolk
1 tablespoon minced
   parsley or chives

Simmer asparagus in salted water until tender (10 to 20 minutes). Drain, reserving the liquid. Brown flour in butter, add drained liquid to it, and simmer for 5 minutes. Blend in cream mixed with egg yolk, and add asparagus. Heat almost to boiling, but do not boil. Before serving, add parsley or chives. Serves 2 to 4.

CREAMED BRUSSELS SPROUTS
KAPUSTOVÁ POUPATA NA SMETANĚ

1½ pounds Brussels
    sprouts
    boiling water to cover
¼ cup butter
1½ tablespoons flour

1⅔ cups cream
salt to taste
pepper to taste
dash of mace
dash of nutmeg

Soak cleaned Brussels sprouts in cold water for 15 minutes. Drain, then place in boiling water for 5 minutes. Drain again. Melt butter, blend in flour; add cream, and stir until smooth. Add Brussels sprouts, salt, and pepper. Simmer for 10 minutes or until tender. Add mace and nutmeg to taste. Serves 6 to 8.

CABBAGE PATTIES
ZELNÉ KARBENÁTKY

3 slices bacon, chopped
2 cups chopped cooked
    cabbage
2 knockwursts or 4 frank-
    furters, sliced
    salt to taste

1 egg
    bread crumbs as needed
¼ cup flour
½ cup shortening for
    frying

Fry bacon and add to it cabbage, knockwurst or frankfurters, salt, egg, and enough bread crumbs to make a medium firm dough. Shape into patties, roll in flour, and brown in hot shortening. Serves 4.

SAUTÉED CABBAGE
HLÁVKOVÉ ZELÍ DUSENÉ

Bohemian Cabbage
České zelí

1½ pounds cabbage,
    shredded
1 cup water
1 medium onion,
    chopped
½ cup lard

½ teaspoon caraway
    seeds
salt to taste
1–2 teaspoons sugar
    juice of 1 lemon (or
      vinegar to taste)
2 teaspoons flour

Simmer cabbage in water for about 5 minutes. Add onion browned in lard, caraway seeds, and salt, and sauté 10 to 15 minutes. Add sugar, lemon juice or vinegar, and flour; simmer for 5 minutes. Serves 4.

Moravian Cabbage
Moravské zelí

1½ pounds cabbage,
    shredded
1 cup water
1 medium onion,
    chopped
½ cup lard

⅓ cup flour
½ teaspoon caraway
    seeds
salt to taste
4 teaspoons sugar
⅓ cup vinegar

Simmer cabbage in water for 5 minutes. Brown onion in lard, add flour, and stir until brown. Pour in the liquid from cabbage, and stir until smooth. Add cabbage, caraway seeds, salt, sugar, and vinegar. Simmer for 20 minutes. Serves 4.

STUFFED CABBAGE HEAD
ZELNÁ HLAVA PLNĚNÁ

1 head of cabbage
1 medium onion, chopped
¼ cup butter
1 pound ground meat
   (beef, veal, pork, or
   ham)
salt to taste

pepper to taste
1 tablespoon minced
   parsley
1 egg, lightly beaten
½–1 cup water or stock
   melted butter

Remove stump from cleaned cabbage. Scoop out and chop inside of cabbage, leaving about a 1- or 1½-inch-thick shell. Wilt onion in 2 tablespoons of the butter. Add meat; brown. Add chopped cabbage, salt, pepper, and parsley. Sauté for 10 minutes. Cool. Stir egg into cooled mixture and fill cabbage shell with it. Cover the opening with a cabbage leaf and fasten with toothpicks. Place in a deep casserole, add 2 tablespoons butter, and ½ cup water or stock. Cover, and cook for 1 hour. Add more water as needed. To serve, cut in wedges and pour on melted butter. Serves 4 to 6.

SAUTÉED ÇARROTS
MRKEV DUŠENÁ

3 cups sliced carrots
1 cup water
½ cup butter
   salt to taste
½ teaspoon sugar

3 tablespoons flour
1 cup milk
   juice of ½ lemon
1 tablespoon minced
   parsley or chives

Cook carrots in water with butter, salt, and sugar until tender (15 to 25 minutes). Dust with flour, add milk, and simmer for 5 minutes. Before serving, add lemon juice and parsley or chives. Or cook carrots with green peas, kohlrabi, asparagus tips, or fresh mushrooms. Serves 4 to 6.

FRIED CAULIFLOWER
KVĚTÁK SMAŽENÝ

1 2-pound cauliflower	1 egg, lightly beaten
salt to taste	⅔ cup flour
½ cup milk	shortening for frying

Break cauliflower into flowerets and cook for 5 to 10 minutes in boiling salted water. Drain. Beat together milk, egg, and flour. Dip drained flowerets into mixture, and fry in deep fat to a golden brown. Serves 4 to 6.

CAULIFLOWER SOUFFLÉ
KVĚTÁKOVÝ NÁKYP

1 cup butter	1 cup cooked and
salt to taste	chopped veal or ham
4 eggs, separated	¼ teaspoon nutmeg
1 cup sautéed mushrooms	2 tablespoons minced
2 cups cooked cauliflower,	parsley
separated into	2 cups (approximately)
flowerets	bread crumbs

Cream ½ cup butter; add salt and egg yolks, mix well. Add mushrooms, cauliflower, meat, nutmeg, parsley, and 1⅔ cups bread crumbs; blend well. Fold in stiffly beaten egg whites. Pour into a greased baking dish lightly dusted with bread crumbs. Bake in a hot-water bath in a preheated 350° oven for 45 minutes. Brown ¼ cup bread crumbs in remaining ½ cup butter and sprinkle over casserole before serving. Serves 4 to 6.

CAULIFLOWER WITH EGGS (MOCK BRAINS)
KVĚTÁK S VEJCI (NEPRAVÝ MOZEČEK)

1 medium onion, chopped	salt to taste
¼ cup butter	dash of powdered caraway seeds
1½ cups chopped cooked cauliflower	1 tablespoon minced chives
4 eggs, lightly beaten	

Fry onion in butter, add cauliflower, and heat thoroughly. Add eggs, salt, and caraway seeds, stirring until eggs are set. Sprinkle with chives before serving. Serves 2 to 3.

BOILED CELERY ROOT
CELER VAŘENÝ

2 large celery roots (2 pounds)	salt to taste
	¼ cup vinegar

Scrub celery roots well with a stiff brush. Boil in salted water with vinegar for 20 to 40 minutes, or until tender. Drain, plunge into cold water; peel and slice. Serve with Hollandaise Sauce or Homemade Mayonnaise (see Index). Or use in a vegetable or potato salad. Serves 4.

FRIED CELERY ROOT
CELER SMAŽENÝ

2 large celery roots (2 pounds)	⅔ cup flour
salt to taste	1–2 eggs, lightly beaten
water	1 cup bread crumbs
¼ cup vinegar	1 cup shortening for frying

Clean and peel celery root; slice into pieces about ¾ inch thick. Simmer in salted water with vinegar 2 to 5 minutes.

Drain and pat dry. Dip in flour, then egg, then bread crumbs. Fry in shortening until golden brown. Serves 3 to 4.

CUCUMBER STUFFED WITH MEAT
OKURKY PLNĚNÉ MASEM

½ pound veal, cut up
1 medium onion
1 bay leaf
3 peppercorns
1 tablespoon butter

1 egg
½ cup bread crumbs
4 cucumbers
¼ cup chopped bacon

Simmer meat with onion and seasonings until tender. Remove meat from pan and grind. Add butter, egg, and bread crumbs. Blend. Pare and cut cucumbers lengthwise into halves. Hollow out centers, fill with meat mixture, and cook in bacon until tender (about 30 minutes). Serves 3 to 4.

GREEN BEANS PAPRIKA
FAZOLOVÉ LUSKY NA PAPRICE

1 medium onion, chopped
¼ cup butter
¼ teaspoon paprika
1 pound green beans cut into 1-inch pieces (3 cups)

salt to taste
½ cup water
2 tablespoons flour
½ cup sour cream

Fry onion in butter, add paprika, beans, salt, and water. Simmer until tender (20 to 30 minutes). Mix flour with sour cream, stir into beans. Simmer for 5 minutes. Serve with meat or hard-cooked eggs and potatoes. Serves 4.

BOILED KALE
KAPUSTA VAŘENÁ

1 (1-pound) head of kale	½ cup bread crumbs
water to cover	½ cup butter
salt to taste	

Boil head of kale in salted water for 15 to 20 minutes, uncovered. Drain and quarter; sprinkle with bread crumbs browned in butter. This may also be served with Mushroom or Anchovy Sauce (see Index). Serves 4.

SAUTÉED KALE
KAPUSTA DUŠENÁ

¼ cup chopped bacon	⅓ cup flour
1 medium onion, chopped	1–1½ cups water
2 small (1½-pound)	salt to taste
heads of kale,	pepper to taste
cut into strips	

Fry onion with bacon. Add kale and sauté until tender (10 to 15 minutes). Dust with flour, add water, salt, and pepper. Simmer for 5 minutes. Serves 4 to 6.

KALE PATTIES
KAPUSTOVÉ KARBANÁTKY

1 pound kale	1 egg
2 rolls	2 tablespoons flour
1 medium onion, grated	1¼ cups (approximately)
salt to taste	bread crumbs
pepper to taste	⅔ cup shortening

Boil kale in salted water for 10 minutes. Drain. Soak rolls in water and squeeze dry. Chop kale and rolls together finely, or grind. Add onion, salt and pepper, egg, flour, and enough bread crumbs to make a soft dough. Form into patties, roll in the remaining bread crumbs, and brown in shortening. Serves 4.

KALE WITH EGGS (MOCK BRAINS)
KAPUSTA S VEJCI (NEPRAVÝ MOZEČEK)

1 medium onion, chopped	salt to taste
¼ cup butter	4 eggs, lightly beaten
1 (1-pound) head of kale, cut into strips	

Fry onion in butter; add kale, sprinkle with salt, and sauté until tender (10 to 15 minutes). Add eggs and stir until set. Serves 2 to 4.

STUFFED KALE ROLLS
KAPUSTOVÉ ZÁVITKY

2 small heads of kale, boiled	FILLING
¼ cup butter	1 pound cooked pork, ground
½ cup stock	½ pound cooked smoked meat, ground
	2 cups cooked rice
	salt to taste
	marjoram to taste
	1½ cups chopped mushrooms
	2 tablespoons butter

Sauté mushrooms in 2 tablespoons butter. Blend together all ingredients for filling. Pull off kale leaves carefully; chop the hearts and add to filling. Put 2 tablespoons filling on each kale leaf; roll up. Arrange in a greased baking dish, dot with butter, pour in stock. Bake in a preheated 375° oven for 30 to 45 minutes. Serves 4 to 6.

BOILED KOHLRABI
BRUKEV VAŘENÁ

8 kohlrabi (2 pounds),
  peeled and sliced
2 cups water

salt to taste
¼ cup bread crumbs
¼ cup butter

Boil kohlrabi in salted water 15 to 20 minutes. Drain. Brown bread crumbs in butter. Sprinkle over kohlrabi. Serves 6 to 8.

KOHLRABI BAKED WITH HAM
BRUKEV ZAPEČENÁ SE ŠUNKOU

½ cup butter
8 kohlrabi, diced
  salt to taste
½ pound ham, chopped
1 tablespoon minced
  parsley

3 egg yolks
1 cup cream
2 tablespoons flour
  salt to taste
  pepper to taste
  dash of mace

Melt 6 tablespoons butter; add kohlrabi and salt. Sauté for 10 minutes. Grease a baking dish with the remaining butter. Put in a layer of kohlrabi, sprinkle with part of ham and parsley. Repeat layers, ending with kohlrabi. Mix egg yolks with cream, flour, salt, pepper, and mace. Pour over kohlrabi. Bake in a preheated 350° oven for about 30 minutes. Serves 4.

KOHLRABI KRAUT
BRUKVOVÉ ZELÍ

1 medium onion, chopped
¼ cup butter
8 kohlrabi (2 pounds),
  peeled and cut into
  thin strips

pinch of caraway seeds
salt to taste
1 tablespoon flour
½ cup water
vinegar to taste
sugar to taste

Fry onion in butter; add kohlrabi, caraway seeds, and salt. Sauté for 10 to 15 minutes. Dust with flour; add water, vinegar, and sugar; bring to a boil, and serve. Serves 6 to 8.

SAUTÉED KOHLRABI ·
BRUKEV DUŠENÁ

8 kohlrabi (2 pounds), peeled and sliced	2 tablespoons flour
⅓ cup butter	½ cup milk or stock
salt to taste	1 tablespoon minced parsley or dill

Sauté kohlrabi in butter, sprinkle with salt. When done, dust with flour and add milk or stock. Bring to a boil. Before serving, add parsley or dill. Serves 6 to 8.

LENTILS
ČOČKA NA KYSELO

1½ cups lentils	¼ cup lard
3–4 cups water	2 tablespoons flour
1 medium onion, chopped	salt to taste
	2 tablespoons vinegar

Wash lentils and soak in water overnight. Cook until soft (about 1 hour). Fry onion in half the lard; add flour, and stir until brown. Add 1 cup water, bring to a boil, and add to lentils. Salt to taste. Simmer for 5 to 10 minutes. Add vinegar and the remaining lard. Serve with poached or boiled eggs. Serves 4 to 6.

SAUTÉED MUSHROOMS
DUŠENÉ HOUBY

1 medium onion,
   chopped
⅓ cup butter

1 pound mushrooms,
   sliced
½ teaspoon caraway seeds
   salt to taste

Fry onion in butter; add mushrooms, caraway seeds, and salt. Sauté for 10 to 15 minutes. Serves 4.

MUSHROOMS WITH SOUR CREAM
HOUBY NA SMETANĚ

Prepare Sautéed Mushrooms (above). Blend in 1 tablespoon flour mixed in ½ cup sour cream. Simmer for 5 minutes. Serves 4.

PICKLED MUSHROOMS
HOUBY V OCTĚ

2 pounds mushrooms
⅓ cup vinegar
1 cup water
   salt to taste
1 teaspoon sugar

3 peppercorns
2 allspice
1 small bay leaf
   pinch of mustard seeds

Simmer small whole or large quartered mushrooms in salted water for 3 minutes. Drain. In another pot, simmer vinegar, the cup of water, salt, sugar, peppercorns, allspice, and bay leaf for 5 minutes. Cool. Arrange mushrooms in a screw-top jar and sprinkle with mustard seeds. Pour the strained vinegar mixture over them. Cover, and store in a cool place for about 1 week. Serves 20.

MUSHROOMS WITH EGGS
HOUBY S VEJCI

1 pound mushrooms,
   sliced
   salt to taste

⅓ cup butter
4 eggs, lightly beaten

Place mushrooms and salt in a pan and cook until all the liquid evaporates (10 to 15 minutes). Add butter, and when it is melted, add eggs. Scramble together and serve. Serves 2 to 4.

PEAS WITH BARLEY
HRÁCH A KROUPY

2 cups cooked dried peas
2 cups cooked barley
¼ cup lard

1 medium onion,
   chopped
8–12 slices bacon, fried

Mix freshly cooked peas with barley and lard. Brown onion in bacon drippings. Sprinkle crumbled bacon and onion over the peas with barley. Serve with boiled smoked meat and pickles. Serves 4 to 6.

CREAMED GREEN PEAS
HRÁŠEK NA SMETANĚ

1 pound (2 cups shelled)
   fresh green peas
½ cup salted boiling water
¼ cup butter
½ teaspoon sugar
   salt to taste

pepper to taste
dash of nutmeg
1 cup cream
2 tablespoons flour
1 tablespoon minced
   parsley

Simmer peas in water for 5 minutes. Drain. Sauté with butter and sugar until tender (5 to 15 minutes). Stir in seasonings and cream mixed with flour; simmer for 3 minutes. Before serving, add parsley. Serves 4.

SAUTÉED GREEN PEAS
HRÁŠEK DUŠENÝ

1 pound (2 cups shelled) fresh peas	1 tablespoon flour
½ cup salted boiling water	½ cup milk or stock
¼ cup butter	1 tablespoon minced parsley

Simmer peas in water for 5 minutes. Drain. Sauté in butter until tender (5 to 15 minutes). Dust with flour, stir in milk or stock. Bring to a boil, add parsley.

Peas may also be sautéed with other vegetables: carrots, kohlrabi, cauliflower, lettuce hearts, etc. Serves 2 to 3.

STUFFED GREEN PEPPERS
PAPRIKY PLNĚNÉ

8 green peppers, cleaned

FILLING

1 medium onion, chopped
2 tablespoons shortening
1 pound ground pork, or pork and beef
1 tablespoon minced parsley
salt to taste
pepper to taste
1 cup cooked rice

SAUCE

2 large onions, chopped
⅓ cup oil
1 pound tomatoes, chopped
salt to taste
½ cup sour cream

To prepare filling, sauté onion in shortening. Add meat, parsley, salt, and pepper. Brown meat. Remove from heat and add rice. Stuff the peppers with the mixture.

To prepare sauce, sauté onion in oil. Add tomatoes. Cook for 20 minutes. Rub through a sieve and add salt. Place stuffed peppers in the sauce, cover, and simmer for 30 minutes. Before serving, add sour cream to sauce. Serves 4 to 6.

GREEN PEPPERS WITH MEAT AND RICE
PAPRIKY ZAPEČENÉ S MASEM A RÝŽÍ

3 medium onions, sliced
½ cup shortening
½ pound pork, diced
½ pound lamb, diced
salt to taste

1 pound tomatoes, sliced
8 green peppers, sliced
1 cup uncooked rice
1–2 cups water or stock

Fry 1 onion in ¼ cup of shortening, add meat and salt, and brown. In another pan, sauté tomatoes in the remaining shortening for 20 to 30 minutes. Rub through a sieve, and add to meat. Add last 2 onions, green peppers, and rice. Put mixture into a greased casserole, add water or stock, and bake in a preheated 350° oven until rice is tender (45 to 60 minutes). Serves 4.

GREEN PEPPERS AND TOMATOES
PAPRIKY DUŠENÉ S RAJČATY

2 medium onions, sliced
¼ cup shortening
8 green peppers, cut into
   strips

8 hard tomatoes, sliced
salt to taste
pepper to taste
4 eggs

Sauté onion in shortening, add green peppers, and cook for 10 minutes. Add tomatoes, salt, and pepper and cook for 10 to 15 minutes longer. Add eggs, and stir until they are set. Serve with rolls or bread. Serves 4.

SAUTÉED GREEN PEPPERS
PAPRIKY JAKO "MINUTKA"

8 green peppers, cut into
   strips
¼ cup shortening

salt to taste
dash of ground caraway
   seed

Add peppers to shortening with salt and caraway seed. Cook, covered, about 7 minutes. Serve with rolls, bread, or fried potatoes. Serves 4 to 6.

MOCK FRENCH FRIES
BRAMBORY SMAŽENÉ NA PEKÁČI

2 pounds potatoes, peeled
   and sliced
⅓ cup lard

1 teaspoon salt
pinch of caraway seeds

Melt lard on a 4-sided baking sheet. Place potatoes on top in a single layer. Sprinkle with salt and caraway seeds. Bake in a preheated 350° oven for 30 to 40 minutes or until brown, turning over once. Serves 6 to 8.

POTATO AND EGG CASSEROLE
BRAMBORY ZAPÉKANÉ S VEJCI

2 pounds potatoes,
   cooked, peeled, and
   sliced
3–4 hard-cooked eggs,
   chopped

1 cup grated hard cheese
½ cup butter, melted
   salt to taste
1 cup milk
1 raw egg

Arrange a layer of potatoes in a greased casserole; sprinkle with chopped cooked eggs, cheese, butter, and salt. Repeat process once. Beat raw egg lightly, mix with milk; pour over casserole. Bake in a preheated 350° oven for 20 to 30 minutes, or until eggs are set. Serves 4 to 6.

POTATO AND MUSHROOM CASSEROLE
BRAMBORY ZAPÉKANÉ S HOUBAMI

1 medium onion, chopped	¼ teaspoon caraway seeds
½ cup butter	2 pounds cooked potatoes,
2 pounds mushrooms,	peeled and sliced
sliced	1 cup milk
salt to taste	2 eggs, lightly beaten

Sauté onion in butter, add mushrooms, salt and caraway seeds. In a greased casserole arrange alternate layers of potatoes and mushrooms. Repeat layering, ending with potatoes. Mix together milk and eggs, and pour over casserole. Bake in a preheated 350° oven for 20 to 30 minutes, or until eggs are set. Serves 4 to 6.

POTATO GOULASH WITH MARJORAM
BRAMBOROVÝ GULÁŠ S MAJORÁNKOU

1 medium onion,	salt to taste
chopped	¼ cup flour
¼ cup shortening	¼ cup shortening
2½ pounds potatoes,	gravy seasoning (see
peeled and sliced	Explanatory Notes)
water to cover	or soy sauce to taste
½ teaspoon marjoram	

Fry onion in half the shortening; add potatoes, water, marjoram, and salt. Cook until tender. Stir in flour browned in remaining shortening; simmer for 5 to 10 minutes. Add gravy seasoning or soy sauce. Serves 6.

POTATO GOULASH WITH PAPRIKA
BRAMBOROVY GULÁŠ NA PAPRICE

2 medium onions,
   chopped
½ cup lard or chopped
   bacon
½ teaspoon paprika
   dash of pepper
¼ teaspoon caraway
   seeds

2½ pounds potatoes,
   peeled and sliced
salt to taste
water as needed
½ cup cream
1 tablespoon flour

Fry onions in lard or bacon; add paprika, pepper, caraway seeds, potatoes, and salt. Half cover with water. Cook until potatoes are tender. Mix cream with flour, stir into potatoes, and simmer for 5 minutes. Serve as is, or with any leftover diced meat, fish, vegetables, or hard-boiled eggs added. Serves 6.

POTATO CONES
BRAMBOROVÉ ŠIŠKY

1 recipe Potato
   Dumplings I (see
   Index)

1 cup bread crumbs
½ cup shortening

Prepare dough. Roll into cones 1 inch by 2½ inches. Boil in salted water for 4 minutes. Drain. Brown bread crumbs in shortening, add cones, and stir. Serve with meat, or as a meatless meal with vegetables or salad. Serves 4 to 6.

POTATO MUSH
ŠKUBÁNKY

2½ pounds potatoes,
   peeled and
   quartered
   boiling salted water to
   cover
1½ cups instantized flour

salt to taste
½ cup lard, melted
½ cup poppy seeds,
   ground
½ cup sugar

Pour water over potatoes. Cook until done. Drain, reserving about half the water. Mash the potatoes. Make wells in potatoes with the handle of a wooden spoon, and fill with flour. Pour in the reserved drained water, cover, and bring to a boil. Turn off heat, but let pot stand covered for 20 minutes. Mix into very firm dough. Dip a large spoon in lard and scoop out mixture by spoonfuls; place on a plate, one mound next to the other. Pour the remaining lard over the mounds, and sprinkle with poppy seeds and sugar. Serves 4 to 6.

POTATO PANCAKES (RAW POTATOES)
BRAMBORÁK

2½ pounds potatoes	1–2 eggs
salt to taste	1 cup flour
milk as needed	¾ cup shortening

Peel and grate potatoes, drain (measuring liquid drained off), and sprinkle with salt. Add milk (about the same amount as drained-off liquid) to potatoes, eggs, and flour; mix well. Drop pancake batter by spoonfuls into hot shortening and fry to a golden brown. Serves 4 to 6.

POTATO PATTIES
BRAMBOROVÉ SMAŽENKY

1 recipe Potato Dumplings II (see Index)	1 cup bread crumbs
2 eggs, beaten	¾ cup shortening

Prepare dough according to instructions, but omit croutons. Roll out ½ inch thick, and cut into 2½-inch circles. Dip in eggs, roll in bread crumbs, and brown in hot shortening. Serve with roasts, or as a meatless meal with vegetables. Serves 4 to 6.

POTATO POCKETS
BRAMBOROVÉ TAŠTIČKY

1 recipe Potato
Dumplings I (see
Index)
1½ cups Prune Butter Fill-
ing or Poppy Seed
Filling (see Index)

¼ cup butter, melted
½ cup grated
gingerbread

Prepare dough according to instructions. Roll out ¼ inch thick and cut into 3-inch squares. Place 1 tablespoon prune butter or poppy seed filling in center of each square and fold over into a triangle. Seal the edges. Boil in salted water for 5 minutes. Drain. Serve sprinkled with butter and gingerbread. Makes about 16 to 20 pockets.

POTATO ROLL
BRAMBOROVÝ ZÁVIN

1 recipe Potato
Dumplings I (see
Index)
½ cup bread crumbs,
browned in
2 tablespoons shortening
1 onion, chopped,
browned in
2 tablespoons shortening

2 cups diced, cooked,
smoked meat
¼ cup bread crumbs,
browned in
¼ cup shortening

Prepare dough. Roll into a rectangle ¾ inch thick. Sprinkle with ½ cup browned bread crumbs, onion, and meat. Roll up tightly. Wrap in a large wet napkin, tie at both ends. Boil in salted water for 40 minutes. Remove from water and unroll carefully from napkin. Slice and arrange on a plate. Sprinkle with ¼ cup browned bread crumbs. Serves 4 to 6.

FRANKFURTERS IN BLANKETS
PÁRKY V TĚSTĚ

1 recipe Potato　　　　　　　(see Index)
　Dumplings II　　　　　10–12 frankfurters

Prepare dough according to instructions, but omit croutons. Roll out dough ½ inch thick. Cut frankfurters into halves, wrap dough around each half, and seal. Brown in hot shortening. Serves 6.

POTATOES AND BARLEY
NASTAVOVANÁ KAŠE

⅔ cup barley　　　　　　　2 pounds potatoes, peeled
1 cup water or milk　　　　1 medium onion, chopped
2 tablespoons shortening　　¼ cup butter
1 teaspoon salt

Cook barley in water or milk, shortening, and salt, until tender (45 minutes). Boil potatoes in water to cover; drain and mash. Mix barley and potatoes; brown onion in butter and pour it over mixture. Serves 4 to 6.

SAUTÉED POTATOES
BRAMBORY DUŠENÉ VE VLASTNÍ ŠŤÁVĚ

3 pounds potatoes, peeled　　1 tablespoon minced
　and sliced　　　　　　　　parsley or chives
2 cups diced cooked meat　　salt to taste
½ cup lard

Arrange alternate layers of potatoes, meat, lard, and parsley in a greased flameproof casserole. Finish with a layer of potatoes and lard. Cover tightly and sauté over a low flame until tender (45 to 60 minutes). Serves 4 to 6.

POTATOES SAUTÉED WITH VEGETABLES
BRAMBORY DUŠENÉ SE ZELENINOU

Potatoes with Kale
S kapustou

1 medium onion, chopped
½ cup chopped bacon
1 pound kale, chopped
1 pound potatoes, peeled
and diced
salt to taste

pepper to taste
water to cover
1 tablespoon flour
gravy seasoning (see
Explanatory Notes)
or soy sauce to taste

Fry onion in bacon, add kale, potatoes, salt, and pepper, and sauté for a few minutes. Add water and simmer until tender (about 20 minutes). Dust with flour, add gravy seasoning or soy sauce, and simmer for 5 minutes. Serves 2 to 4.

Potatoes with Tomatoes
S rajskými jablíčky

1 medium onion, chopped
¼ cup oil
1 pound potatoes, peeled
and diced
1 pound tomatoes, peeled
and sliced

salt to taste
pepper to taste
1 tablespoon minced
parsley

Fry onion in oil, add potatoes, and sauté for 10 minutes. Add tomatoes, salt, and pepper; cover, and simmer until tender. Before serving, add parsley. Serves 2 to 4.

BAKED POTATOES WITH CHEESE
BRAMBORY PLNĚNÉ SÝREM

8 medium baking potatoes
½ cup butter
2 egg yolks
½ cup grated cheese
salt to taste
¼ teaspoon paprika

½ cup sour cream
2 tablespoons grated
cheese
1 tablespoon minced
parsley

Bake potatoes in a 450° oven until done (about 45 minutes). Cut a thin slice off, lengthwise; scoop out the inside and mash. Cream butter and egg yolks. Add the ½ cup cheese, mashed potato, salt, paprika, and sour cream. Mix well, and refill the potato shells. Sprinkle with cheese and parsley, and bake in a 350° oven for 30 minutes. Serves 4 to 8.

BAKED POTATOES WITH MEAT
BRAMBORY PLNĚNÉ MASEM

8 medium baking potatoes
salt to taste
pepper to taste
2 cups diced cooked meat
1 medium onion, chopped
2 tablespoons butter
½ cup butter, melted
¼ cup grated cheese
1 tablespoon minced
parsley

WHITE SAUCE

3 tablespoons flour
2 tablespoons butter
½ cup milk

Bake potatoes in a 450° oven until done (about 45 minutes). Cut a thin slice off each, lengthwise, and scoop out the inside. Mash, add salt and pepper, meat, white sauce, and onion fried in 2 tablespoons butter. (To prepare sauce, melt butter, blend in flour; add milk gradually, stirring constantly until mixture thickens.) Refill potato shells and arrange in a baking dish. Pour ½ cup butter over all, sprinkle with cheese and parsley. Bake in a 350° oven for 30 minutes. Serve with vegetables. Serves 4 to 8.

BAKED POTATOES WITH EGGS
BRAMBORY PLNĚNÉ VEJCI

5 baking potatoes	salt to taste
¼ cup butter, melted	1 tablespoon minced
5 eggs	parsley

Bake potatoes in a 450° oven until done (about 45 minutes). Cut a thin slice off each potato, lengthwise, and scoop out about half the inside. Brush inside with butter. Break an egg into each potato, sprinkle with salt and parsley. Bake in a 350° oven until eggs are set (20 to 35 minutes). Serves 5.

SOUR POTATOES
BRAMBORY NA KYSELO

2½ pounds potatoes, peeled and sliced	1 cup sour cream
salted water to cover	1 tablespoon vinegar
½ teaspoon caraway seeds	½ teaspoon sugar
¼ cup flour	1 tablespoon chopped dill or chives
¼ cup shortening	1 or 2 egg yolks

Boil potatoes in salted water with caraway seeds. Drain, and reserve liquid. Brown flour in shortening, stirring constantly, and stir in 1 to 1½ cups of potato water. Simmer for 10 to 15 minutes. Add the remaining ingredients and potatoes. Serve as is, or add diced boiled meat. Serves 6.

SAUTÉED SAUERKRAUT
DUŠENÉ KYSELÉ ZELÍ

1 medium onion, chopped	2 tablespoons flour
¼ cup lard	1 tablespoon sugar
1 pound sauerkraut	salt to taste
½ teaspoon caraway seeds	½ cup white wine or water

Brown onion in lard. Add sauerkraut and caraway seeds, and sauté until tender (30 to 45 minutes). Dust with flour, sugar, and salt. Stir in wine or water, and simmer for 5 minutes. Serves 3 to 4.

SPINACH SOUFFLÉ I
ŠPENÁTOVÝ NÁKYP

3 eggs, separated	½ pound ham or smoked
½ cup butter	meat, chopped
salt to taste	pepper to taste
2 hard rolls	1 clove garlic, mashed
½ cup milk	melted butter
3 cups cooked spinach,	grated cheese
chopped	

Cream egg yolks with butter and salt. Soak rolls in milk, and rub through a sieve. Add to butter mixture. Add remaining ingredients. Fold in stiffly beaten egg whites. Bake in a greased soufflé form in a preheated 350° oven 30 to 35 minutes, or until eggs are set. Serve with melted butter and grated cheese. Serves 6 to 8.

SPINACH SOUFFLÉ II
ŠPENÁTOVÝ NÁKYP

2 pounds spinach,	salt to taste
cleaned	¾ cup flour
3 tablespoons butter	⅔ cup grated cheese
2 eggs, separated	pepper to taste
¼ cup heavy cream	nutmeg to taste

Steam spinach 3 to 5 minutes. Drain and chop fine. Cream butter and egg yolks; add cream, salt, flour, cheese, seasonings, and spinach. Mix well. Fold in stiffly beaten egg whites. Put in a greased casserole and bake in a preheated 350° oven for about 30 minutes, or until eggs are set. Serves 4 to 6.

SPINACH OMELET

OMELETA SE SÝROVÝM ŠPENÁTEM

4 eggs, separated
2 teaspoons hot water
½ pound fresh spinach,
  cleaned and chopped

salt to taste
2 teaspoons cold water
¼ cup butter

Beat egg yolks with salt and hot water. Add spinach. Add cold water to egg whites, beat until stiff; fold into yolk-spinach mixture. Grease 2 frying pans well with butter, and pour half the batter into each. Bake in a preheated 350° oven for about 30 minutes, or until eggs are set. Serves 2.

SPINACH PUDDING

ŠPENÁTOVÝ PUDINK

2 pounds spinach,
  cleaned
4 eggs, separated
2 rolls
1⅓ cups milk

salt to taste
dash of mace
¼ cup butter
2 tablespoons bread
  crumbs

Soak rolls in milk. Steam spinach for 3 to 5 minutes. Drain and grind. Beat egg yolk until creamy, add rolls, salt, mace, and spinach. Fold in stiffly beaten egg whites. Grease a covered pudding form well, sprinkle with bread crumbs. Pour in mixture, cover, and cook in a pan of boiling water for about 45 minutes. Serve with melted butter and fried bread crumbs. Serves 4 to 6.

SPINACH PANCAKES

ŠPENÁTOVÉ LÍVANEČKY

1 pound spinach, cleaned
¼ cup butter
2 eggs, separated

salt to taste
⅓ cup flour

Steam spinach 3 to 5 minutes. Drain and chop very fine.

Cream butter with egg yolks, add salt, spinach, and flour. Mix well. Fold in stiffly beaten egg whites. Bake on a greased griddle. Make pancakes small (about 3 inches in diameter). Serves 4 to 6.

TOMATOES WITH EGGS I
OPEČENÁ RAJČATA S VEJCI

4–6 slices Canadian bacon	4–6 eggs
1 medium onion, sliced	salt to taste
1 pound tomatoes, sliced	pepper to taste

Brown bacon in a frying pan. Top each slice with onion and tomatoes. Cook 10 to 15 minutes, or until all the liquid evaporates. Place an egg on each slice; cover, and cook slowly until eggs are set. Serves 4 to 6.

TOMATOES WITH EGGS II
OPEČENÁ RAJSKÁ JABLÍČKA S VEJCI

4 ounces bacon (about 8 slices)	salt to taste
	pepper to taste
1 large onion, sliced	1 tablespoon minced
1 pound tomatoes, sliced	parsley
4–6 eggs	

Fry bacon in a skillet, add onion slices, and brown lightly. Add tomato slices, and cook until all the liquid evaporates. Break in eggs, sprinkle with salt and pepper, cover, and cook until eggs are set. Serve sprinkled with parsley. Serves 4 to 6.

TOMATOES WITH A WARM MEAT FILLING
RAJSKÁ JABLÍČKA S TEPLOU MASITOU NÁDIVKOU

16 medium tomatoes
salt to taste
lemon juice to taste
½ cup butter
1 large onion, chopped
2 cups diced cooked meat
2 cups cooked rice

½ cup cooked mush-
rooms
salt to taste
pepper to taste
1–2 eggs, lightly beaten
¼ cup grated cheese
or bread crumbs

Cut off tops of tomatoes, reserve. Scoop out insides, and sprinkle with salt and lemon juice. Brown onion in half the butter, add meat, rice, mushrooms, salt, and pepper, and heat thoroughly. Stir in eggs. Fill tomatoes with this mixture, sprinkle with cheese or bread crumbs, dot with butter, and replace the tops. Put tomatoes into a greased casserole, and bake in a preheated 350° oven for 30 to 40 minutes. Serves 4 to 8.

FRIED TOMATOES
RAJSKÁ JABLÍČKA SMAŽENÁ

½ cup white wine or water
2 eggs, separated
⅔ cup flour

salt to taste
5 firm tomatoes, sliced
shortening for frying

Mix wine, egg yolks, flour, and salt. Fold in stiffly beaten egg whites. Dip tomatoes in mixture; fry to a golden brown. Serve with mashed potatoes. Serves 2 to 4.

TOMATOES FILLED WITH
EGGS AND CHEESE
RAJSKÁ JABLÍČKA PLNĚNÁ VEJCI A SÝREM

8 tomatoes
  salt to taste
  pepper to taste
1 cup grated Swiss or
  American cheese

¼ cup butter
8 eggs
1 tablespoon minced
  parsley

Cut out a circle at the stem end in tomatoes. Scoop out insides carefully, sprinkle with salt, pepper, and half of the cheese. Put in a bit of butter, and drop an egg into each tomato. Sprinkle with more salt, the remaining cheese, and parsley. Bake in a preheated 350° oven for 30 minutes or until eggs are set. Excellent as a meatless dish with potato or legumes purée. Serves 4 to 8.

VEGETABLE SOUFFLÉ
ZELENINOVÝ NÁKYP PEČENÝ

2½ cups diced vegetables
  (cauliflower, aspara-
  gus, green peas, car-
  rots, kohlrabi, etc.)
1 cup diced cooked
  potatoes
½ cup sliced mushrooms

1 cup diced ham or
  smoked meat
2 tablespoons grated
  cheese
½ cup butter, melted
1 cup cream or milk
1 egg
1 tablespoon flour

In a greased casserole, place a layer each of vegetables, potatoes, mushrooms, and ham. Sprinkle with cheese and butter. Repeat. Bake in a preheated 350° oven for 10 minutes. Mix together egg and flour; add cream. Pour over the casserole. Bake 20 minutes longer. Serves 6 to 8.

SALADS AND SALAD DRESSINGS

SMOKED HERRING SALAD
SALÁT Z UZENÁČŮ

½ pound smoked herring,
    boned and diced
½ pound potatoes, cooked
    and diced

1 small onion, chopped
1 cup mayonnaise
    lemon juice to taste

Blend all ingredients. Mound in lettuce cups. Serves 4.

ITALIAN SALAD
VLAŠSKÝ SALÁT

2 cups ham, cut into strips
2 cups cooked, peeled
    potatoes, cut into strips
2 cups pickles, cut into
    strips
1 cup onion, cut into strips

1 cup sour apples, cored,
    peeled, and cut into
    strips
    salt to taste
    pepper to taste
    Homemade Mayonnaise
    (see Index)

Place meat, potatoes, pickles, onions, and apples in a bowl. Add salt and pepper, mix, and bind with mayonnaise. Chill for several hours. Serves 8 to 10.

RUSSIAN SALAD
RUSKÝ SALÁT

3 cups diced ham	1 pickled herring, diced
2 cups diced cooked potatoes	1 tablespoon capers
1 cup peas	salt to taste
1½ cups diced pickles	pepper to taste
1 cup diced onion	Homemade Mayonnaise (see Index)

Mix all ingredients with salt and pepper. Bind with mayonnaise and chill for several hours. Serves 8 to 10.

PRAGUE SALAD
PRAŽSKÝ SALÁT

1½ cups thin strips of roast veal	1 cup thin strips of sour apples
1½ cups thin strips of roast pork	salt to taste
1½ cups thin strips of pickles	pepper to taste
1 cup thin strips of onion	1 tablespoon lemon juice
	Homemade Mayonnaise (see Index)

Mix together cut-up ingredients. Sprinkle with lemon juice, salt, and pepper; bind with mayonnaise. Chill for several hours. Serves 8.

CARROT SALAD WITH APPLES
MRKVOVÝ SALÁT S JABLKEM

2 cups shredded carrots	salt to taste
2 cups shredded apples	¼ cup sugar
juice and peel (grated) of 2 lemons	

Toss all ingredients together and serve immediately. Oranges may be substituted for lemons. Serves about 4.

MIXED SALAD
MÍCHANÝ SALÁT

2 pounds cooked potatoes,
 peeled and diced
½ cup cooked peas
½ cup diced cooked celery
 root
½ cup diced, cooked
 carrots and parsnip

2 pickles, diced
1 cup diced ham
1 medium onion,
 chopped
1 tablespoon capers
1 hard-cooked egg,
 chopped
1–1½ cups mayonnaise

Toss together all ingredients. Chill and serve. Serves 6 to 8.

COOKED CELERY ROOT SALAD
CELEROVÝ SALÁT

2 large celery roots (2
 pounds)
1½ cups boiling water
¼ cup vinegar

salt to taste
1 small onion, chopped
3 tablespoons oil
pepper to taste

Clean and peel celery root. Quarter, and cut into thin slices. Simmer in salted water with vinegar for 15 to 20 minutes. Pour into a bowl, add salt, onion, oil, and pepper. Chill (liquid will jell when cool), and serve. Serves 4.

RAW CELERY ROOT SALAD
SALÁT ZE SYROVÉHO CELERU

1 large (1 pound) celery
 root
½ small onion, chopped

¼ cup mayonnaise
1 tablespoon lemon juice

Clean, peel, and grate celery root. Add onion, and toss with mayonnaise and lemon juice. This may also be used as a sandwich spread. Serves 2.

GREEN BEAN SALAD
SALÁT Z FAZOLOVÝCH LUSKŮ

3 cups cooked green beans,
    cut into 1-inch pieces
1 large onion, chopped

DRESSING

½ cup water
2 tablespoons vinegar
1 tablespoon oil
    salt to taste
½ teaspoon sugar
OR
⅔ cup mayonnaise
lemon juice to taste

Toss together all ingredients, chill, and serve. Serves about 4.

CAULIFLOWER SALAD
SALÁT Z KVĚTÁKU

SALAD

3 cups cauliflower,
    broken into flower-
    ets
4 cups water
    ¯salt to taste
1 bay leaf
3—4 peppercorns

DRESSING

½ cup water
3 tablespoons vinegar
    salt to taste
½ teaspoon sugar
1 small onion, grated
3 tablespoons oil

Boil cauliflower in salted water with bay leaf and pepper-corns for about 10 minutes. Drain. Mix dressing, pour over flowerets, and chill. Serves about 4.

KOHLRABI SALAD
BRUKVOVÝ SALÁT

8 small young kohlrabi,
   peeled and grated

DRESSING

½ cup water
2 tablespoons vinegar
1 tablespoon oil
  salt to taste
½ teaspoon sugar
   OR
⅔ cup mayonnaise

Toss together all ingredients. Serves 4.

LETTUCE WITH BACON
HLÁVKOVÝ SALÁT SE SLANINOU

2–3 heads Boston
   lettuce
½ cup water
½ teaspoon sugar

¼ teaspoon salt
2 tablespoons vinegar
3–4 strips bacon,
   chopped and fried

Wash lettuce and break up into a bowl. Dissolve sugar and salt in water, add vinegar, and pour over lettuce. Before serving, pour warm, not hot, bacon and fat over the salad. Serves 4 to 6.

LETTUCE WITH SOUR CREAM
HLÁVKOVÝ SALÁT S KYSELOU SMETANOU

2–3 heads Boston
   lettuce
1 cup sour cream

¼ teaspoon salt
½ teaspoon sugar
2 tablespoons vinegar

Wash lettuce and break up into a bowl. Mix the remaining ingredients and pour over lettuce. Toss. Serves 4 to 6.

ONION SALAD
CIBULOVÝ SALÁT

1 cup water
½ cup vinegar
1 pound onions, sliced

DRESSING

2 tablespoons oil
1–2 tablespoons vinegar
salt to taste
¼ teaspoon sugar

Bring water and vinegar to a boil. Add onions, bring again to full boil. Drain. Mix dressing, pour over onions. Chill. Serves 3 to 4.

PARSNIP SALAD
SALÁT Z PASTINÁKU

1⅓ cups water
⅔ cup vinegar
2 peppercorns
2 allspice
2 cloves
1 bay leaf

salt to taste
1 pound parsnips, pared
and sliced
boiling water to cover
1–2 tablespoons oil
1 large onion, chopped

Bring water with vinegar, spice, and salt to a boil. In another pot, pour fresh boiling water over parsnips; simmer for 2 minutes. Drain parsnips, place in boiling vinegar water, cover, and simmer for about 30 minutes. Remove spice, add oil. Chill. Before serving, sprinkle onion over top. Serves 4 to 6.

GREEN PEPPER AND TOMATO SALAD
SALÁT Z PAPRIK A RAJČAT

2 green peppers (½
  pound), sliced
2 tomatoes (½ pound),
  sliced
2 medium onions (½
  pound), sliced
  salt to taste

⅔ cup water
⅓ cup vinegar
1 peppercorn
1 allspice
1 bay leaf
  sprig of dill

Mix tomatoes, peppers, and onions; sprinkle with salt. Simmer water, vinegar, and spices together for 5 to 10 minutes. Cool, strain, and pour over vegetables. Serves 4.

PLAIN POTATO SALAD
OBYČEJNÝ BRAMBOROVÝ SALÁT

2 pounds potatoes, boiled,
  peeled, and diced

2 medium onions, chopped
3 pickles, chopped

DRESSING

¾ cup water
4 tablespoons oil
½ teaspoon mustard
½ teaspoon sugar
2 tablespoons lemon juice
  salt to taste
  pepper to taste

OR

1 cup beef stock, warm
2 tablespoons vinegar
  salt to taste
  pepper to taste
  sugar to taste

Mix potatoes, onions, and pickles. Add either dressing, and toss. Serves 6 to 8.

POTATO SALAD WITH MEAT (OR FISH)
SALÁTY BRAMBOROVÉ MASITÉ

2 pounds potatoes, cooked
and diced
1 large onion, chopped
3 sour-sweet pickles,
diced
salt to taste

vinegar to taste
½ pound (1½ cups)
diced meat (any
kind) or fish
¾–1 cup mayonnaise, to
taste

Mix all ingredients well. Chill. Serves 6 to 8.

POTATO SALAD WITH VEGETABLES
BRAMBOROVÝ SALÁT SE ZELENINOU

2 pounds potatoes, cooked,
peeled, and diced
2 medium onions, chopped
2 pickles, chopped
1 cup peas, or 2 cups diced
green peppers
and tomatoes

2 apples, diced, or ½
cup chopped
sauerkraut
1–1½ cups mayonnaise

Toss all ingredients together well. Chill and serve. Serves
6 to 8.

RADISH SALAD
SALÁT Z ŘEDKVIČEK

1 pound radishes
juice of 1 lemon
1 tablespoon water

½ teaspoon sugar
salt to taste
1 tablespoon oil

Grate radishes coarsely. Mix all other ingredients, and pour
over radishes. Toss well. Chill before serving. Serves 6 to 8.

CREAM SALAD DRESSING
SMETANOVÁ SALÁTOVÁ OMÁČKA

¼ cup water
¼ cup lemon juice or
  vinegar
2 egg yolks

salt to taste
2 tablespoons butter
1 cup sour cream

Mix together water, lemon juice or vinegar, egg yolks, and salt. Heat in a double boiler, beating with a wire whisk until thickened. Remove from heat, add butter. Cool. Blend in sour cream. Makes about 1½ cups.

PLAIN SALAD DRESSING
SALÁTOVÁ ZÁLIVKA S OCTEM

½ cup water
½ teaspoon salt
1 teaspoon sugar

1–2 tablespoons vinegar
pepper to taste
2 tablespoons oil

Dissolve salt and sugar in water. Add the remaining ingredients; mix well. Makes about 1 cup.

SOUR CREAM SALAD DRESSING
SALÁTOVÁ OMÁČKA Z KYSELÉ SMETANY

1 cup sour cream or sour
  milk
½ teaspoon salt
½ teaspoon sugar

1 tablespoon lemon juice or
  vinegar
pepper to taste

Dissolve salt and sugar in sour cream or milk. Add remaining ingredients; mix well. Makes about 1 cup.

BREAD, ROLLS AND COFFEE CAKES

Explanatory Notes

SINGLE-ACTING BAKING POWDER

Phosphate type, is not very successfully interchanged with double-acting (sodium aluminium sulphate) baking powder. If a recipe calls for single-acting baking powder, and you want to substitute double-acting baking powder for it, use ¼ less.

COMPRESSED (FRESH) YEAST

Compressed yeast seems to give more satisfactory results in the recipes in this book than does granular yeast, but if you cannot obtain compressed yeast, use granular, bearing in mind that 2 ounces (4 tablespoons) compressed yeast is equal to 4 packages dry or granular yeast. Follow the directions on the package for dissolving granular yeast (remember that a warmer liquid—110° to 115°—is needed to dissolve granular than fresh yeast); then proceed as directed in the recipe.

Whether you are using compressed or granular yeast, *be sure it is fresh*. Always dissolve compressed yeast before using to test its freshness; fresh yeast will foam and bubble in 5 to 10 minutes. Granular yeast carries on the package a date beyond which it should not be used for best results. Note that in many of the recipes here, sugar is crumbled over the yeast and the two mixed together until the sugar liquefies.

To be successful with yeast dough, you must give it special attention. Not only must the yeast be fresh, but the ingredients—and even the bowl in which you mix the dough—must be lukewarm or at least at room temperature. And, finally, let the dough rise in a warm place, free from drafts.

INSTANTIZED FLOUR

This is the nearest to the "00"-type European flour used in the original recipes, and does not contain as much gluten as all-purpose flour.

PÂTÉ SPICE

GINGERBREAD SPICE

GRAVY AND SOUP SEASONING

CRYSTAL SUGAR

SUGAR WAFER SHEETS

WHITE WAFER SHEETS

POPPY SEEDS

Most of the above products are not available in regular stores and supermarkets; they are imported by and sold in special stores. One such store, filled with all kinds of fascinating imported merchandise, is: H. ROTH & SON (LEKVAR-BY-THE-BARREL), at 1577 First Avenue, corner of 82nd Street, New York, N.Y. 10028. Their catalogue is available on request, and they ship mail orders everywhere.

SOFT YEAST DOUGH
POLOTUHÉ TĚSTO KYNUTÉ

1 tablespoon compressed yeast (see Explanatory Notes)	¼ cup sugar
	1 teaspoon salt
	1 cup lukewarm milk
1 tablespoon sugar	¼ cup butter, melted
2 tablespoons flour	1 egg
2 tablespoons lukewarm milk	½ teaspoon grated lemon peel
4 cups flour	1 teaspoon vanilla

Place yeast in a bowl, sprinkle yeast with sugar, and stir until mixture liquefies. Add 2 tablespoons flour and 2 tablespoons milk; blend. Cover with a cloth and let rise in a warm place for 5 to 10 minutes. Add all other ingredients; mix well with a wooden spoon. Remove dough from bowl, put on a floured pastry board, and knead until it is smooth and does not stick. Return to bowl, sprinkle with flour, and cover with a cloth. Let it rise in a warm place (about 80°F.) 30 to 60 minutes or until it is almost doubled. Punch down, form into desired shapes and let rise again for about 30 minutes. Bake in a preheated oven at 400° for 15 to 20 minutes.

FIRM YEAST DOUGH I
TUHÉ KYNUTÉ TĚSTO

5½ teaspoons compressed yeast (see Explanatory Notes)	1 cup lukewarm milk
	½ cup butter, melted
	2 egg yolks
1 tablespoon sugar	½ teaspoon grated lemon peel
2 tablespoons flour	1 teaspoon vanilla
2–3 tablespoons lukewarm milk	¼ cup raisins
4½ cups flour	⅓ cup Blanched Almonds (see Index), sliced
½ cup sugar	2 tablespoons chopped citron
1 teaspoon salt	

Follow directions for making Soft Yeast Dough (above). This dough will take longer to rise because it is much richer. Add raisins, almonds, and citron after dough has been kneaded. Form into desired shapes and bake in a preheated oven at 400° for 15 to 20 minutes.

FIRM YEAST DOUGH II
TUHÉ KYNUTÉ TĚSTO

2 tablespoons plus ½
   teaspoon
   compressed yeast
   (see Explanatory
   Notes)
1 tablespoon sugar
2 tablespoons flour
2–3 tablespoons
   lukewarm milk
4½ cups flour
⅔ cup sugar
1 teaspoon salt

1 cup (approximately)
   lukewarm milk
⅔ cup butter, melted
3–4 egg yolks
½ teaspoon grated
   lemon peel
1 teaspoon vanilla
½ cup raisins
½ cup Blanched
   Almonds (see
   Index), sliced
⅓ cup chopped citron

Follow directions for making Soft Yeast Dough (see Index). This dough will take longer than Soft Yeast Dough to rise because it is much richer. After kneading the dough, add raisins, almonds, and citron. Form into desired shapes and bake in a preheated oven at 400° for 15 to 20 minutes.

YEAST DOUGH STRUDEL
ZÁVIN

1 recipe Yeast Puff
   Dough (see Index)

2–3 cups Poppy Seed or
   Apple Filling (see
   Index)
1 egg, beaten

Prepare dough; roll out into 2 rectangles ¼ inch thick. Spread with filling and roll up. Put on a buttered baking sheet (seam side down), and let rise. Brush with egg, and bake in a preheated 350° oven for 30 to 45 minutes. Sprinkle with sugar. Serves 4.

BOHEMIAN BISCUITS
VDOLKY

1 recipe Soft Yeast
   Dough (see Index)

Prepare dough; roll out about ¾ inch thick. Cut into 3- to 4-inch rounds and place on a buttered baking sheet. Let rise. Bake in a preheated 400° oven for about 10 minutes or until bottoms of biscuits are brown; turn over and let brown on other side (about 10 minutes more).

Served warm spread with prune or blueberry jam, sprinkled with cottage cheese, and topped with a spoonful of sour cream.

YEAST DOUGH FOR MINIATURE ROLLS
KYNUTÉ TĚSTO NA DROBNÉ SLANÉ PEČIVO

2 teaspoons compressed
   yeast (see
   Explanatory Notes)
¼ teaspoon sugar
1 tablespoon flour
4–5 tablespoons lukewarm
   milk
2 cups flour

2 tablespoons grated
   cheese
salt to taste
½ cup butter, melted
1 egg white, lightly beaten
   coarse salt
   caraway seeds or poppy
   seeds

Mix yeast with sugar until mixture liquefies; add the 1 tablespoon flour, and milk. Let rise until bubbly (5 to 10 minutes). Stir in the 2 cups flour, cheese, salt, and butter. Knead into a firm dough. Let rise in a warm place, covered, until double in bulk. Punch down. Shape into small rolls, sticks, or pretzels, and place on a greased baking sheet. Let rise again. Brush with egg white, and sprinkle with coarse salt and caraway or poppy seeds. Bake in a preheated oven at 400° for 15 to 20 minutes.

LOMNITZ BISCUITS
LOMNICKÉ SUCHÁRKY

1 tablespoon
  compressed yeast
  (see Explanatory
  Notes)
1 teaspoon sugar
1 tablespoon flour
2–3 tablespoons
  lukewarm milk

2⅔ cups flour
¾ cup butter
⅓ cup Blanched
  Almonds (see
  Index), chopped
1–2 cups Vanilla Sugar
  (see Index)

Stir yeast and sugar together until mixture liquefies; add the tablespoon flour, and milk. Let rise 5 to 10 minutes (until bubbly). Cut butter into the 2⅔ cups flour, then add raised yeast mixture. Work into a firm dough. Let rise, covered, in a warm place for 1 hour. Punch down. Add almonds. Shape into a roll 1½ inches thick. Place on a greased baking sheet and let rise again for 1 hour. Bake in a preheated 350° oven for 20 to 30 minutes. Next day, cut roll into slices about ¼ inch thick, and roll in Vanilla Sugar. Dry on a baking sheet.

CRISP POTATO DOUGH STICKS
KŘEHKÉ TĚSTO S BRAMBORY

¾ cup grated cooked
  potatoes
1⅓ cups flour
¾ cup shortening
  salt to taste

1 egg, lightly beaten
  coarse salt
  caraway seeds }(optional)
  grated cheese

Work potatoes, flour, shortening, and salt into a smooth dough. Roll out about ¼ inch thick. Cut into sticks with a pastry wheel. Brush with egg, and sprinkle with coarse salt and caraway seeds, or grated cheese. Bake in a preheated 400° oven for about 15 minutes.

BUTTER LEAF CRESCENTS
LOUPÁČKY

1 recipe Salt Rolls (see   ½ cup butter, melted
    Index)   1 egg, beaten

Prepare dough. Roll out ¼ inch thick and cut into long triangles. Brush generously with melted butter and roll up, beginning at the wide end. Shape into crescents on a buttered baking sheet and let rise. Brush with egg and bake in a preheated 400° oven for 15 to 20 minutes.

YEAST DOUGH ROLLS
ZÁVIN

1 recipe Soft Yeast   2–3 cups Cheese or
    Dough (see Index)   Poppy Seed Filling
                            (see Index)
                        1 egg, beaten

Prepare dough; roll out into 2 rectangles ¼ inch thick. Spread with filling and roll up. Put on a buttered baking sheet (seam side down), and let rise. Brush with egg and bake in a preheated 350° oven for about 30 to 45 minutes. Serves 4.

LOMNITZ RINGS AND PRETZELS
LOMNICKÉ VĚNEČKY A PRECLÍČKY

1 recipe Lomnitz   1–2 cups Vanilla Sugar
    Biscuits dough (see   (see Index)
    Index)

Shape dough into ¼-inch-thick rolls. Twist into rings or pretzels. Let rise, covered, in a warm place on a greased baking sheet. Bake in a preheated 350° oven for 15 to 25 minutes. Roll in Vanilla Sugar.

SALT ROLLS
HOUSKY

2 tablespoons plus 1
    teaspoon compressed
    yeast (see Explanatory
    Notes)
1 tablespoon sugar
2 tablespoons flour
2–3 tablespoons
    lukewarm milk

$4\frac{1}{4}$ cups flour
2 teaspoons salt
1 egg
$\frac{1}{2}$ cup lukewarm milk
$\frac{1}{4}$ cup butter, melted

TOPPING

1 egg, beaten
    coarse salt

whole poppy seeds or
    caraway seeds (optional)

Prepare dough as in recipe for Soft Yeast Dough (see Index), and, after it has risen, punch down and shape into long sticks or small rolls. Or roll dough out and cut it into strips ½ inch wide and 6 inches long; braid 3 strips and press ends together. Place on a greased baking sheet and let rise. Brush with egg and sprinkle with coarse salt, and add poppy seeds or caraway seeds, if you like. Bake in a preheated 400° oven for 15 to 20 minutes.

BRIOCHES
BRIOŠKY

1 recipe Firm Yeast
    Dough I or II (see
    Index)

1 egg, beaten

Knead raised dough on lightly floured board and shape into buns. Place on a well-greased baking sheet and let rise again. Cut a cross in top of each with scissors; brush with egg. Bake in a preheated 400° oven for 15 minutes; reduce heat to 375° and bake for 10 to 15 minutes longer.

FILLED CRESCENTS
ROHLÍKY MARTINSKÉ

1 recipe Soft Yeast
   Dough (see Index)

2 cups Nut or Poppy Seed
   Filling (see Index)
1 egg, beaten

Prepare dough; roll out about ¾ inch thick. Cut into 3- to 4-inch rounds and place on a buttered baking sheet. Let roll up from the straight end toward the point. Shape into crescents on a buttered baking sheet, and let rise. Brush with egg and bake in a preheated 350° oven for 30 to 40 minutes.

CABBAGE ROLLS
ZELNÍKY

1 recipe Soft Yeast
   Dough (see Index)
¼ cup butter, melted

FILLING

4 cups shredded cabbage
2 tablespoons butter
salt to taste
sugar to taste
½ teaspoon vanilla
¼ cup milk

Stew cabbage in butter for about 10 minutes. Add the remaining ingredients, and cook for 10 minutes longer or until all liquid has evaporated. Cool. Roll out dough about ¾ inch thick, and cut into 4-inch squares. Place a spoonful of filling in the center of each. Bring dough edges together and pinch to seal in filling. Place rolls on a buttered baking sheet, and let rise. Brush with melted butter. Bake in a preheated 350° oven for about 30 minutes.

SWALLOWS
VLAŠTOVKY

1 recipe Firm Yeast Dough I or II (see Index)	1 egg, beaten

Knead raised dough on lightly floured board. Cut into strips 5 inches by ¾ inch. Tie a knot in each, and cut the ends a few times with a knife or scissors. Place on a well-buttered baking sheet, and let rise again. Brush with egg. Bake in a preheated 400° oven for 15 minutes; reduce heat to 375° and bake 10 minutes longer.

YEAST PUFF DOUGH
PŘEKLÁDANÉ TĚSTO KYNUTÉ
(PLUNDROVĚ)

BUTTER DOUGH

1¼ cups butter
1 cup flour

YEAST DOUGH

4½ teaspoons compressed yeast (see Explanatory Notes)	3 cups flour
	1 teaspoon salt
1 tablespoon sugar	¼ cup sugar
2 tablespoons flour	2 eggs
3 tablespoons lukewarm milk	1 egg yolk
	½ cup lukewarm milk

Prepare Butter Dough first. Cut butter into flour; work to a dough. Shape into a rectangle ½ inch thick. Put into refrigerator.

To make Yeast Dough, mix yeast with sugar until it liquefies. Add flour and milk; mix well. Let rise in a warm place for 5 to 10 minutes (until bubbly). Add other ingredients and beat with a wooden spoon until dough loosens from spoon. Cover with a cloth and let rise in a warm place for about 1 hour. Place Yeast Dough on a floured pastry board and roll out into a square. Place Butter Dough in the center of Yeast Dough and fold Yeast Dough over it, like an envelope, pinching corners together in the center. Fold in half and roll out into a rectangle about ½ inch thick. Fold lower third up over center third, and fold remaining third down over first third. Fold in half again, bringing the 2 shorter sides together. Cover and let rest for 1 hour in a cool place, then roll out and repeat folding process. Let rest for another 30 minutes. Roll out and form into desired shapes, place on a greased baking sheet, and let rise again. Bake in a preheated oven at 400° for 15 to 20 minutes.

PRETZELS
PRECLÍKY

1 recipe Yeast Puff Dough (see Index)	1 egg, beaten White Icing (see Index)

Prepare dough; roll out ¼ inch thick. Cut into 10-inch-long, ½-inch-wide strips; twist into pretzels. Place on a buttered baking sheet. Let rise in a warm place. Brush with egg, and bake in a preheated 400° oven for 10 to 15 minutes. Cool, then decorate with White Icing.

COCKSCOMBS
KOHOUTÍ HŘEBENY

1 recipe Yeast Puff Dough (see Index) 2 cups (approximately)	Cheese, Poppy Seed, Nut, or other filling (see Index) 1 egg, beaten

Prepare dough; roll out ¼ inch thick. Cut into rectangles 3 by 5 inches. Lay a strip of filling down the long center of each rectangle, bring the sides together, and seal. Make about six ½-inch cuts on the side opposite the seal. Place Cockscombs on a buttered baking sheet, shaping them into crescents. Let rise in a warm place until almost double in bulk. Brush with egg. Bake in a preheated 400° oven for 10 minutes, then reduce heat to 375° and bake 20 to 30 minutes longer.

EASTER CAKE
BOCHÁNEK VELIKONOČNÍ

1 recipe Firm Yeast Dough I or II (see Index) 1 egg, beaten	2 tablespoons sliced Blanched Almonds (see Index)

Knead prepared raised dough on lightly floured board and shape into a large round loaf. Put on a well-greased baking sheet and let rise. Brush with egg. Cut a cross in top of loaf with scissors; sprinkle with almonds. Bake in a preheated 400° oven for 15 minutes; reduce heat to 375°, and bake 30 to 45 minutes longer.

CHRISTMAS TWIST
VÁNOČKA

1 recipe Firm Yeast Dough I or II (see Index) 1 egg, beaten	2 tablespoons sliced Blanched Almonds (see Index) confectioners' sugar

Knead prepared raised dough on lightly floured board. Divide into 3 large pieces and 5 smaller ones. Roll each piece into a long roll. Braid the 3 larger rolls loosely, and pinch ends together. Place on a well-buttered baking sheet. Braid 3 of the smaller rolls, pinch ends together, and place on the large braid. Twist the last 2 rolls together and place on top, tucking ends under the large braid. Cover with a cloth and let rise 1 to 1½ hours in a warm place. Brush with egg and sprinkle with almonds. Bake in a preheated 400° oven for 15 minutes; reduce heat to 375° and bake for 30 to 45 minutes longer. Sprinkle with sugar.

CROWN CAKE
BÁBOVKA

1 recipe Soft Yeast
   Dough (see Index)
⅓ cup raisins
⅓ cup sliced Blanched
   Almonds (see Index)

2 tablespoons chopped
   citron or candied
   orange peel

Prepare dough, and after it has been kneaded, mix in raisins, almonds, and citron or orange peel. Butter and flour a large fluted tube pan. Place dough in it, cover with a cloth, and let rise in a warm place. Bake in a preheated 350° oven for 45 to 60 minutes. Test cake with a toothpick before removing from oven. When it is done, let it stand in pan for 5 minutes, then turn out on a wire rack to cool. (If cake sticks to pan, wrap outside of pan in a damp towel for a few minutes.) Sprinkle with sugar.

FESTIVAL BUNS
POSVÍCENSKÉ KOLÁČE

1 recipe Soft Yeast
   Dough (see Index)
2–3 cups Cheese, Poppy
   Seed, Apple, Prune
   Butter, or other
   filling (see Index)

1 egg, beaten
   confectioners' sugar

Prepare dough. Roll out raised dough on lightly floured board to about ½-inch thickness. Cut into 3-inch rounds and place on buttered baking sheet. Press down center of rounds with bottom of a 2-inch glass to form a hollow; place a spoonful of filling in each. Let rise again. Brush edges of rounds with egg. Bake in a preheated 400° oven for 20 to 30 minutes. When buns are cool, sprinkle with sugar. Makes 2½ to 3 dozen.

MORAVIAN BUNS
KOLÁČE MORAVSKÉ

1 recipe Soft Yeast
 Dough
1–1½ cups Cheese Filling
 (see Index)
1–1½ cups Prune Butter,
 Poppy Seed, or
 Apple Filling
 (see Index)

1 egg, beaten
Crumb Topping
 (see Index)
confectioners' sugar

On lightly floured board, roll out raised dough to about ½-inch thickness. Cut into 3-inch rounds. Place a teaspoonful of Cheese Filling in the center of each, pinch dough edges together, shape into a ball, and place on a buttered baking sheet. Make an indentation in the center of each bun and put in a spoonful of the second filling you are using. Let rise again. Brush with egg and sprinkle with Crumb Topping. Bake in a preheated 400° oven for 30 to 40 minutes. Sprinkle with sugar when cool.

BOHEMIAN BUNS I
KOLÁČE ŠÁTEČKOVÉ ČESKÉ

1 recipe Soft Yeast
 Dough (see Index)
2–3 cups Cheese, Poppy
 Seed, or Prune
 Butter Filling (see
 Index)

1 egg, beaten
Crumb Topping (see
 Index)
confectioners' sugar

On lightly floured board, roll out raised dough about ½ inch thick. Cut into 3- or 4-inch squares. Put a heaping spoon of filling in the center of each. Pull out corners of dough slightly and pinch together over center. Place buns on a buttered baking sheet and let rise. Brush with egg and sprinkle with Crumb Topping. Bake in a preheated 400°

oven for 25 to 30 minutes. When buns are cool, sprinkle with sugar.

BOHEMIAN BUNS II
ŠÁTEČKOVÉ KOLÁČE

1 recipe Yeast Puff
  Dough (see Index)
2–3 cups Cheese, Poppy
  Seed, Apple, or
  other filling (see
  Index)

1 egg, beaten
  confectioners' sugar

On lightly floured board, roll out dough ½ inch thick. Cut into 3- to 4-inch squares. Put a heaping spoon of filling in the center of each. Pull out corners slightly and press together over center. Place on a buttered baking sheet and let rise. Brush with egg. Bake in a preheated 400° oven for 25 to 30 minutes. When buns are cool, sprinkle with sugar.

YEAST DOUGH CAKE I
KOLÁČ NA PLECH

½ recipe Soft Yeast
  Dough (see Index)
2–3 cups Cheese, Poppy
  Seed, Apple, or
  Prune Butter Filling
  (see Index)

OR

2 pounds (approximately)
  fresh fruit (pitted
  cherries, fresh prunes,
  or apricots, or sliced
  peaches, blueberries,
  etc.)
1 egg, beaten
  confectioners' sugar

Prepare dough. With floured hands, spread raised dough onto a 4-sided buttered baking sheet. Press dough against sides of pan to form a ½-inch-high rim. Cover dough with filling or fruit; let rise. Brush edges with egg. Bake in a preheated oven at 350° for 30 to 50 minutes. When cake is cool, sprinkle with sugar and cut into serving pieces.

YEAST DOUGH CAKE II
KOLÁČE SKLÁDANÉ DOMAŽLICKÉ

½ recipe Soft Yeast
    Dough (see
    Index)
½–¾ cup each of Cheese,
    Poppy Seed,
    Prune Butter, and
    Apricot Jam
    filling (see
    Index)

1 egg, beaten
    confectioners' sugar

On lightly floured board, roll out dough into 2 circles the width of a baking sheet. Place each on a buttered baking sheet, and turn edges up to make a rim ½ inch high. Spread with fillings: either spread a different filling on each quarter of the disks, or make concentric circles of the fillings on the dough. Let rise. Brush dough edges with egg and bake in a preheated 350° oven for 30 to 50 minutes. When cakes are cool, sprinkle with sugar.

FILLED SUGAR BUNS
BUCHTY

1 recipe Soft Yeast
    Dough (see
    Index)
2–2½ cups Cheese, Poppy
    Seed, Prune
    Butter, or other
    filling (see
    Index)

⅔–1 cup butter,
    melted
    confectioners' sugar

Place raised dough on floured pastry board. Cut into pieces about 3 by 4 by ¾ inches. Put a heaping spoonful of filling in the center of each; bring the 2 shorter edges together, and pinch to seal in filling on 3 sides. Grease a large oblong cake pan with butter. Place buns in, side by side, brushing well with butter in between and on top of them. Let rise for 30 minutes. Bake in a preheated 350° oven for 30 to 45 minutes. Turn out carefully on a wire rack to cool. Separate buns, and sprinkle with sugar. Makes about 24 to 30 buns.

JELLY DOUGHNUTS
KOBLIHY

4½ teaspoons compressed yeast	pinch of salt
1 tablespoon sugar	1–2 tablespoons rum
2 tablespoons flour	1 cup (approxi-
3 tablespoons lukewarm milk	mately) milk or cream
3 tablespoons butter	1 cup jam (apricot,
¼ cup sugar	raspberry, or
4–5 egg yolks	currant)
4¼ cups flour	1½–2 cups oil for frying
	confectioners' sugar

Blend yeast and the tablespoon of sugar together until mixture liquefies, add flour and milk, and beat well. Put in a warm place, cover, and let rise 5 to 10 minutes. Beat butter with sugar and egg yolks until foamy. Mix in raised yeast. Add flour, salt, rum, and enough milk to make a medium firm dough. Beat with a wooden spoon until smooth; dough will then loosen from spoon. Dust with flour, cover, and let rise in a warm place for about 45 minutes. On a lightly floured board, roll out dough lightly about ⅛ inch thick. Cut out circles with a 3-inch cutter. Put 2 teaspoons of jam in the center of half the dough circles, cover with the remaining circles; press edges together with fingertips, and cut doughnuts again with cutter to trim dough. Place doughnuts on a warm floured cloth, cover with a napkin, and let rise for about 15 minutes. Turn over, and let rise again for 15 minutes. Heat ¾ inch of oil in a skillet, put doughnuts in, and cover immediately. Shake skillet slightly a few times during cooking so doughnuts do not stick to bottom. Fry about 2 or 3 minutes, turn with a spatula, and fry on the other side, uncovered. Remove from pan and drain on absorbent paper. A light border should show around the middle. Dust with sugar. Makes about 2 dozen doughnuts.

COOKIES AND COOKIE FILLINGS

FOUNDATION COOKIES I
SUŠENKY

4 cups flour
¾ cup sugar
1¼ cups butter

4 egg yolks, or 2 eggs
1 teaspoon vanilla

Sift flour with sugar onto a pastry board. Cut in butter. Add eggs and vanilla, and work into a smooth dough. Roll out ⅛ to ³⁄₁₆ inch thick. Cut into desired shapes, and bake in a preheated 350° oven for about 10 minutes.

All three types of Foundation Cookies (I, II, and III) can be decorated with icings (see Index), or put together in pairs with jams or cookie fillings (see Index), or served just plain.

FOUNDATION COOKIES II
SUŠENKY

4½ cups flour
2 teaspoons single-acting
baking powder (see
Explanatory Notes)
¾ cup sugar

½ cup butter
2 eggs
5 tablespoons milk
1 teaspoon vanilla

Sift flour with baking powder and sugar. Cut in butter, add eggs, milk, and vanilla, and work into a smooth dough. Roll out on a floured board ⅛ inch thick. Cut cookies into desired shapes, and bake on a greased cookie sheet in a preheated 350° oven for about 10 minutes. Decorate or fill (see above) as you wish.

156

FOUNDATION COOKIES III
SUŠENKY

2 cups flour	1 cup sugar
2 cups cornstarch	½ cup butter
4 teaspoons single-acting	1 egg
baking powder (see	3–5 tablespoons milk
Explanatory Notes)	1 teaspoon vanilla

Prepare and bake like Foundation Cookies II (above).

BLACK-AND-WHITE LINZ DOUGH
LINECKÉ TĚSTO DVOUBAREVNÉ

2¼ cups flour	1 teaspoon vanilla
½ cup sugar	2 tablespoons (approxi-
¾ cup butter	mately) cocoa
1–2 egg yolks	1–2 egg whites, lightly
	beaten (optional)

Sift flour with sugar. Cut in butter. Add egg yolks and vanilla. Work into a smooth dough. Add cocoa to half the dough. Shape cookies as follows:

I. Checkerboard Cookies
Šachovnice

On a floured board roll out each portion of Linz Dough (above) ½ inch thick. Cut into ½-inch-wide strips. Lay 5 strips alternately on a piece of waxed paper (first a light strip, then a dark, another light, another dark, then a light). The strips must touch each other. Over the first layer place a second layer of strips, this time starting and ending with a dark strip, and top this with a third layer, starting with a light strip. Wrap dough in waxed paper, keeping it flat, and chill for 2 to 3 hours. Slice into ¼-inch-thick cookies, place on a greased baking sheet, and bake in a preheated 350° oven for 10 to 15 minutes.

II. Pinwheels
Závitky

On a floured board roll out each portion of Linz Dough (above) ⅛ inch thick. Brush one with egg white; lay other on top. Roll up, wrap in waxed paper, refrigerate for 2 to 3 hours. Slice cookies ¼ inch thick, and bake on a greased baking sheet in a preheated 350° oven for 10 to 15 minutes.

III. Wheels
Kolečka s obroučkou

On a lightly floured board shape light-colored Linz Dough (above) into a 1-inch-thick roll. Roll out dark dough ⅓ inch thick; brush with egg white, and wrap around light roll. Wrap in waxed paper and chill for 2 to 3 hours. Slice cookies ¼ inch thick, and bake on a greased baking sheet in a preheated 350° oven for 10 to 15 minutes.

IV. Salami Cookies
Salám

Press small leftover pieces of both light- and dark-colored Linz Dough (above) into a 1½- to 2-inch-thick roll. Wrap in waxed paper and refrigerate for 2 to 3 hours. Slice into cookies ¼ inch thick, and bake on a greased baking sheet in a preheated oven at 350° for 10 to 15 minutes.

V. Squares
Řezy ze cytř pruhů

Roll out each portion of Linz Dough (above) ¾ inch thick on a lightly floured board. From each, cut 2 strips ¾ inch wide. Place a light and dark strip next to each other; brush with egg white. On these, place the remaining 2 strips in reverse order. Roll out the rest of the doughs ¼ inch thick. Brush with egg white and wrap around layered strips. Wrap whole in waxed paper and chill for 2 to 3 hours. Slice cookies ¼ inch thick, and bake in a preheated 350° oven on a greased baking sheet for 10 to 15 minutes.

CRISP CHEESE DOUGH STICKS
KŘEHKÉ TĚSTO TVAROHOVÉ

⅔ cup farmer cheese	coarse salt ⎫
1⅓ cups flour	caraway seeds ⎬ (optional)
¾ cup shortening	grated cheese ⎭
salt to taste	
1 egg, lightly beaten	

Mix cheese, flour, shortening, and salt into a smooth dough. Roll out about ¼ inch thick. Cut into sticks with a pastry wheel. Brush with egg, and sprinkle with coarse salt and caraway seeds, or grated cheese. Bake in a preheated 400° oven for about 15 minutes.

BUTTER COOKIES
MÁSLOVÉ PEČIVO

1¼ cups butter	2⅔ cups flour
5 tablespoons sugar	candied fruit and nuts
2 egg yolks	(for decoration)
1 teaspoon vanilla	

Cream butter thoroughly with sugar, egg yolks, and vanilla. Blend in flour. Force through a pastry tube or a cookie press onto an ungreased baking sheet. Decorate with pieces of fruit or nuts, or both. Bake in a preheated 375° oven for 10 to 15 minutes.

CHOCOLATE MOUNDS
COKOLÁDOVÉ HRUDKY

6 tablespoons butter	1 tablespoon potato
6 tablespoons sugar	starch
1 tablespoon cocoa	⅓ cup coarsely chopped
1 teaspoon vanilla	filberts or almonds
1 tablespoon milk	¼ cup rolled oats
	1½ teaspoons butter

Toast oats in 1½ teaspoons butter. Melt the 6 tablespoons butter in a pan; add sugar and cocoa, and heat. Add milk mixed with potato starch, and bring just to boiling point. Remove from heat, and mix in the remaining ingredients. Cool slightly. Shape into small mounds on a flat glass plate or on parchment paper. Put in a cool place to harden.

KARLSBAD RINGS
VĚNEČKY Z VAŘENÝCH ŽLOUTKŮ

¾ cup butter	1 teaspoon grated lemon
½ cup sugar	peel
2 hard-cooked egg yolks,	2½ cups flour
rubbed through a	1 egg, lightly beaten
sieve	½ cup chopped filberts or
2 raw egg yolks	chopped candied
1 teaspoon vanilla	fruit

Cream butter; mix in sugar, egg yolks, vanilla, and lemon peel thoroughly. Add flour. Work into a smooth dough. Roll out on a lightly floured board ⅛ inch thick. Cut into small rings, sprinkle with nuts or fruit. Bake in a preheated 350° oven for 15 to 20 minutes.

COOKIE SQUARES WITH MERINGUE
SUŠENKOVÉ ČTVEREČKY Z DVOJÍHO TĚSTA

COOKIES
2 cups flour
6 tablespoons sugar
½ cup plus 2 tablespoons
    butter
2 egg yolks
½ teaspoon vanilla

MERINGUE
2 egg whites
¾ cup sugar
¾ cup ground Toasted
    Filberts (see Index)

Sift together flour and sugar. Cut in butter. Add egg yolks and vanilla, and work into a smooth dough. Roll out on a lightly floured board to about ¼-inch thickness.

To make meringue, beat egg whites until very stiff, then slowly add sugar, continuing to beat all the while. Fold in filberts. Spread over rolled-out dough. Cut into 1½-inch squares with a knife dipped into cold water, and bake in a preheated 350° oven for 15 to 20 minutes.

JAM-FILLED BALLS
DŮLKOVÉ KOLÁČKY

1 recipe Karlsbad Rings
    dough (see Index)

⅓ cup jam
confectioners' sugar

Prepare dough. Pinch off pieces to make 1½-inch balls. With a wooden spoon handle, make an indentation in the center of each. Bake in a preheated 350° oven for 20 to 25 minutes. Fill centers with jam, and dust with sugar.

COOKIE STICKS WITH YOLK ICING
SUŠENKOVÉ ŘEZY SE
ŽLOUTKOVOU POLEVOU

½ recipe Foundation　　　⅓ cup raspberry jam
　Cookies I, II, or III　　　Yolk Icing (see Index)
　(see Index)

On a lightly floured board, roll out cookie dough into an oblong ¼ inch thick. Bake in a preheated 350° oven for 10 to 15 minutes. Spread a very thin layer of jam on top, and cover with icing. Put into a warm oven for a few minutes to dry. While still warm, cut into strips 2½ inches long and ¾ inch wide.

PARISIAN COOKIES
PAŘÍŽSKÉ PEČIVO

2 eggs　　　　　　　　　chopped candied fruit
½ cup sugar　　　　　　　(optional)
½ cup flour

Combine eggs, sugar, and flour, and beat with a wire whisk for about 10 minutes. Drop by teaspoonfuls on a greased and floured baking sheet. Bake in a preheated 350° oven for 5 to 10 minutes. Remove cookies quickly, one at a time, from the baking sheet, and shape by wrapping around a pencil or wooden spoon handle. Or sprinkle the cookies with chopped candied fruit before baking and do not alter their shape.

CARPENTER'S CURLS
HOBLOVAČKY

½ cup sugar　　　　　　　2 eggs
½ cup flour　　　　　　　1 tablespoon anise seeds

Beat together sugar, flour, and eggs with a wire whisk for about 10 minutes. Grease and flour a baking sheet. With a pastry tube, make 3 or 4 strips of the batter, ½ inch wide, the length of the baking sheet. Sprinkle with anise seeds. Bake in a preheated 350° oven for 5 to 10 minutes. Cut strips into halves or thirds, and curl over the handle of a wooden spoon while still warm. Repeat until all batter is used up.

OATMEAL FLORENTINES
FLORENTÝNKY Z OVESNÝCH VLOČEK

2 cups rolled oats	2 tablespoons flour
¼ cup butter	¼ teaspoon single-acting
6 tablespoons sugar	baking powder (see
1 teaspoon vanilla	Explanatory Notes)
1–2 eggs	

Toast oats in butter in an iron skillet to a golden brown. Cool. Mix flour with baking powder. Add to oats with the remaining ingredients and blend well. Drop from a teaspoon onto a greased and floured baking sheet. Bake in a preheated 350° oven for 10 to 15 minutes.

COCOA OATMEAL COOKIES
KAKAOVÉ HRUDKY Z OVESNÝCH VLOČEK

½ cup butter	1 tablespoon cocoa
½ cup sugar	2½ cups rolled oats
2 eggs, separated	

Cream butter with sugar and egg yolks until foamy. Add cocoa and oats. Fold in stiffly beaten egg whites. Drop from a teaspoon onto a greased baking sheet. Bake in a preheated 350° oven for 15 to 20 minutes.

VANILLA CRESCENTS
VANILKOVÉ ROHLÍČKY

1⅓ cups flour
2 tablespoons sugar
⅓ cup ground almonds or
    filberts
½ cup butter

1 egg yolk
1 teaspoon vanilla
1 cup Vanilla Sugar (see
    Index)
candied fruit
    (optional)

Mix together flour, sugar, and almonds. Cut in butter. Add egg yolk and vanilla, and work quickly into a dough. Chill for about 1 to 2 hours. Shape into small crescents, and bake in a preheated 300° oven for 15 to 20 minutes. Roll in Vanilla Sugar while hot.

This dough may also be shaped into sticks, or into small balls filled with candied fruit, and rolled in Vanilla Sugar.

BEAR PAWS
MEDVĚDÍ TLAPIČKY

3 cups flour
2¼ cups sugar
⅛ teaspoon cinnamon
    pinch of ground cloves
½ cup cocoa

¾ cup ground filberts or
    almonds
1 cup and 3 tablespoons
    butter
1 cup Vanilla Sugar (see
    Index)

Mix together all dry ingredients except Vanilla Sugar. Cut in butter, and work into dough. Break off small pieces and press into greased bear paw molds. Bake in a preheated 350° oven for about 20 minutes. Roll in Vanilla Sugar while still hot.

GINGERSNAPS
ZÁZVORKY

2 eggs
2 egg yolks
1¼ cups sugar
1 teaspoon ginger

2¼ cups flour
⅛ teaspoon powdered
    baking ammonia*

Beat eggs and yolks thoroughly with sugar. Add ginger and flour mixed with ammonia. Roll out dough ⅛ inch thick on a floured board. Cut out cookies and place on a greased baking sheet. Let dry overnight. Bake in a preheated 275° oven 15 to 25 minutes.

GINGERBREAD COOKIES
PERNÍK NA FIGURKY

2⅓ cups flour
1¼ cups sugar
8 teaspoons Gingerbread
    Spice (see Index)
½ teaspoon baking soda
2 tablespoons honey,
    heated to lukewarm

2 eggs, lightly beaten
1 tablespoon rum
1 teaspoon grated lemon
    peel
1 egg, lightly beaten

Sift all dry ingredients onto a pastry board. Add the remaining ingredients except single egg, and work into a firm dough. Let stand overnight in a cool place. Next day, roll out ¼ inch thick. Cut out gingerbread men or any other shapes. Brush with remaining egg. Place on a baking sheet lined with waxed paper and bake in a preheated 325° oven for 20 to 30 minutes. Decorate with icing (see Index).

---

* sold in drugstores as "ammonium carbonate"

COCOA BALLS
KAKAOVÉ DULKOVÉ KOLÁČKY

1 cup flour	5 tablespoons lard, melted
2 tablespoons cocoa	1 teaspoon vanilla
5 tablespoons sugar	⅓ cup jam

Mix together all ingredients except jam into a smooth dough. Form into 1½-inch balls. With the handle of a wooden spoon make an indentation in the center of each. Bake in a preheated 275° oven for 20 to 30 minutes. Fill centers with jam.

MOROCCAN COOKIES
MAROKÁNKY

½ cup milk	⅓ cup sliced Blanched
3 tablespoons sugar	Almonds (see Index)
2 teaspoons butter	⅓ cup sliced candied
2 teaspoons flour	orange peel
	Cocoa Icing (see Index)

Mix together milk, sugar, butter, and flour. Cook over low heat for 1 minute. Add almonds and orange peel. Drop from a teaspoon onto a greased and floured baking sheet. Bake in a preheated 350° oven for 5 to 10 minutes. Remove cookies to wire racks with a spatula and cool flat side up. Spread the flat side with icing.

Cookie Fillings
NÁDIVKY DO ČAJOVEHO PEČIVA

VANILLA FILLING
VANILKOVÁ

½ cup butter
½ cup plus 1 tablespoon
   sugar
1 egg yolk

1 teaspoon vanilla
1⅓ cups Dry Cake Crumbs
   (see Index)

Cream butter with sugar and egg yolk until foamy. Mix in crumbs.

COFFEE FILLING
KÁVOVÁ

6 tablespoons butter
½ cup plus 1 tablespoon
   sugar
1 teaspoon vanilla

1⅓ cups Dry Cake Crumbs
   (see Index)
¼ cup Coffee Flavoring
   (see Index)

Cream butter thoroughly with sugar and vanilla. Add crumbs, sprinkled with Coffee Flavoring; mix well.

COCOA FILLING
KAKAOVÁ

Prepare like Coffee Filling (above), but instead of coffee, use 1 tablespoon cocoa mixed with 2 tablespoons hot water.

RUM OR PUNCH FILLING
RUMOVÁ NEBO PUNČOVÁ

Prepare like Coffee Filling (above), but instead of coffee use ¼ cup rum.

ORANGE OR LEMON FILLING
POMERANCŎVÁ NEBO CITRÓNOVÁ

Prepare like Coffee Filling (above), but use ¼ cup orange or lemon juice instead of coffee.

CHERRY OR APRICOT FILLING
VIŠŇOVÁ NEBO MERUŇKOVÁ

Prepare like Coffee Filling (above), but use only half (or less) the amount of sugar called for, and add enough cherry or apricot sirup or jam instead of coffee to make it right consistency for spreading.

NUT FILLING
OŘECHOVÁ

3 tablespoons sugar	1 cup Dry Cake Crumbs
3 tablespoons water	(see Index)
¾ cup ground nuts	1 tablespoon butter
	1 tablespoon rum

Combine sugar with water and simmer for 5 minutes. Remove from heat, and add the remaining ingredients. Mix well.

FRUIT FILLING
OVOCNÁ

Add chopped candied fruit (dates, figs, orange peel, citron, cherries, etc.) and nuts to a thick jam. Mix in Dry Cake Crumbs (see Index) to desired consistency.

CAKES

POUND CAKE I
TŘENÉ TĚSTO

½ cup butter
½ cup plus 2 tablespoons
sugar
2 eggs, separated
½ teaspoon grated lemon
peel
½ teaspoon vanilla

2 cups instantized flour
6 tablespoons (approxi-
mately) milk
2 teaspoons single-acting
baking powder (see
Explanatory Notes)
fine bread crumbs

Cream butter thoroughly with sugar; add egg yolks, lemon peel, and vanilla, and mix well. Blend in flour and milk alternately by spoonfuls (stir the baking powder into the last ½ cup of flour). Fold in stiffly beaten egg whites. Grease a 9-inch deep cake pan and sprinkle with bread crumbs; pour in batter. Bake in a preheated 350° oven for 35 to 45 minutes.

POUND CAKE II
TŘENÉ TĚSTO

½ cup plus 2 tablespoons
butter
¾ cup sugar
3 eggs, separated
½ teaspoon grated lemon
peel
½ teaspoon vanilla

2 cups instantized flour
6 tablespoons (approxi-
mately) milk
2 teaspoons single-acting
baking powder (see
Explanatory Notes)

Follow instructions for Pound Cake I (above).

169

APPLE CAKE
JABLKOVEC

½ cup butter
¾ cup sugar
4 eggs, separated
4–5 tablespoons milk
3 tablespoons cornstarch
1½ cups instantized flour
2 teaspoons single-acting baking powder (see Explanatory Notes)

7 large apples, pared and sliced thin
cinnamon sugar (3 tablespoons sugar mixed with ½ teaspoon cinnamon)
3 tablespoons butter, melted

Cream butter, sugar, and egg yolks very well. Add milk mixed with cornstarch; blend well. Fold in stiffly beaten egg whites. Sift flour with baking powder; fold in. Spread batter on a greased and lightly floured 4-sided baking sheet. Cover with apples; sprinkle with cinnamon sugar and melted butter. Bake in a preheated 325° oven for 20 to 30 minutes.

CHEESE CAKE
TVAROHOVÝ KOLÁČ TŘENÝ

½ cup butter
½ cup sugar
3 eggs, separated
½ cup cottage cheese, rubbed through a strainer

1 cup ground nuts
⅓–½ cup bread crumbs
jam
grated chocolate
nuts

Cream butter with sugar and egg yolks thoroughly. Blend in cheese and nuts. Fold in stiffly beaten egg whites and bread crumbs. Butter a spring form and sprinkle with bread crumbs. Spread in cake mixture. Bake in a preheated 320° oven for about 30 minutes. When cake is cool, spread with jam and sprinkle with grated chocolate and nuts.

COCOA CAKE
DORT KAKAOVÝ

½ cup plus 2 tablespoons
butter
¾ cup sugar
3 eggs, separated

4 tablespoons cocoa
1 tablespoon hot water
1 teaspoon vanilla
1 cup instantized flour

Cream butter, sugar, and egg yolks until foamy. Add cocoa mixed with hot water and vanilla. Fold in stiffly beaten egg whites, then gently fold in flour. Bake in a greased and floured 9-inch deep cake pan in a preheated 325° oven for 30 to 45 minutes. When cake is cool, split into 2 layers, and fill with Whipped Cream or Vanilla Butter Cream.

CHOCOLATE CAKE I
DORT ČOKOLÁDOVÝ

½ cup butter
½ cup sugar
4 eggs, separated
1 teaspoon vanilla

3½ ounces (squares)
chocolate, melted
1 cup flour

Cream together butter, sugar, and egg yolks until foamy. Add vanilla and chocolate. Gently fold in stiffly beaten egg whites alternately with flour. Pour into greased and floured spring form or 9-inch deep cake pan, and bake in a preheated 325° oven for 30 to 45 minutes. When cake is cool, split into 2 layers and fill with Whipped Cream, or Cocoa or Vanilla Butter Cream.

CHOCOLATE CAKE II
ČOKOLÁDOVÝ DORT Z BÍLKŮ

5 ounces (squares)	8 egg whites
chocolate, melted	¾ cup sugar
5 tablespoons butter	1¼ cups instantized flour

Cream butter with chocolate until foamy. Beat egg whites until very stiff, adding sugar a little at a time, and fold into chocolate mixture. Lightly fold in flour. Pour batter into a greased and floured 9-inch deep cake pan. Bake in a preheated 325° oven for 45 to 60 minutes. Fill like Chocolate Cake I (above).

CHESTNUT CAKE
DORT KAŠTANOVÝ

1 pound chestnuts	1 cup sugar
2 cups milk	6 eggs, separated
6 tablespoons butter	¾ cup grated almonds

To prepare chestnuts, wash them and make incisions on the rounded sides. Roast in a preheated 350° oven for about 15 minutes. Peel. Cook in milk for about 30 minutes. Rub through a strainer while hot, adding to purée whatever liquid has not been absorbed in cooking process, but reserve ¼ cup of the chestnuts for decorating cake.

To prepare cake, cream butter thoroughly with sugar and egg yolks. Add almonds and puréed chestnuts. Fold in stiffly beaten egg whites. Pour into a greased spring form pan sprinkled with bread crumbs. Bake in a preheated 300° oven for 45 to 60 minutes. When cake is cool, split into 2 layers. Fill and cover with Whipped Cream (see Index), and decorate with the ¼ cup chestnuts put through a potato ricer.

CHOCOLATE TREE TRUNK
ČOKOLÁDOVÝ KMEN

6 eggs, separated
6 tablespoons sugar
6 tablespoons instantized
   flour

confectioners' sugar
   (optional)
Chocolate Butter Cream or
   Parisian Cream (see
   Index)

Beat egg whites until very stiff. Add egg yolks, 1 at a time, sprinkling each with sugar, and blend in gently, alternately with spoonfuls of flour. Spread batter ½ inch thick on a greased and floured 4-sided baking sheet. Bake in a preheated 325° oven for 15 to 20 minutes. While hot, roll up in waxed paper or in a damp towel sprinkled with confectioners' sugar. Cool, then unroll and fill with a layer of cream ⅓ inch thick. Roll up again. Spread more cream on top, and, with a fork, draw a design like the bark of a tree. Slice to serve.

BREAD CHERRY CAKE
HOUSKOVÁ BUBLANINA

½ cup butter
½ cup sugar
4 eggs, separated
2⅓ cups (3½ ounces)
   fresh fine bread
   crumbs
2 teaspoons single-acting
   baking powder (see
   Explanatory Notes)

¼ teaspoon cinnamon
1–1½ pounds sour or
   sweet cherries
   confectioners' sugar

Cream butter thoroughly with sugar and egg yolks. Blend in bread crumbs mixed with baking powder and cinnamon. Fold in stiffly beaten egg whites. Spread 1 to 1½ inches high on a greased and floured 4-sided baking sheet. Arrange cherries on top of batter. Bake in a preheated 320° oven for 20 to 30 minutes. Cool. To serve, cut in squares and sprinkle with sugar.

MERINGUE PORCUPINE
SNĚHOVY JEŽEK

CAKE	MERINGUE
5 eggs, separated	3 egg whites
5 tablespoons sugar	¾ cup sugar
5 tablespoons instantized flour	
½ teaspoon vanilla	
1 cup jam	
confectioners' sugar (optional)	

Beat egg whites until very stiff. Add egg yolks, 1 at a time, sprinkling each with sugar, and blending in gently. Fold in flour and vanilla. Spread batter on a greased and floured 4-sided baking sheet. Bake in a preheated 325° oven for 15 to 20 minutes. Turn out onto waxed paper or a damp cloth sprinkled with confectioners' sugar. Spread with jam while still warm, and roll up.

To prepare meringue, beat egg whites until stiff; beat in half the sugar, then fold in the other half. Meringue will be very stiff and glossy.

Place jelly roll on a baking sheet, and with a pastry tube, cover the roll with tiny rosettes of meringue. Bake in a 350° oven for 15 to 20 minutes. Slice to serve.

CHERRY CAKE
TŘEŠŇOVÁ BUBLANINA

1 recipe Pound Cake I or II (see Index)	2 tablespoons (approximately) instantized flour
½–1 pound pitted cherries	fine bread crumbs
	confectioners' sugar

Prepare batter; pour into a large greased cake pan sprinkled with bread crumbs. Spread evenly, 1 to 1½ inches high. Dust cherries with flour and arrange on top of batter. Bake in a preheated 350° oven for 20 to 30 minutes. Cool. To serve, cut into strips and sprinkle with sugar.

RUM FRUIT LOAF
RUMOVÝ CHLEBÍČEK

CAKE	FILLING
4 eggs, separated	4 tablespoons sugar
4 tablespoons sugar	¼ cup water
4 tablespoons instantized	2 tablespoons jam
flour	2 tablespoons rum
	1 tablespoon lemon juice
	½ to 1 cup diced stewed
	or candied fruit
	Water or Fondant Icing
	(see Index)

Beat egg whites until stiff. Add egg yolks, 1 at a time, sprinkling each with sugar and blending in gently. Fold in flour. Pour into a greased and floured 5- by 9-inch loaf pan, and bake in a preheated 325° oven for about 30 minutes. Cool. Cut off a ½-inch layer from bottom of loaf; put rest of cake back into pan, cut side up, and scoop out the inside, leaving a ½-inch-thick shell.

To prepare filling, simmer sugar and water to soft-ball stage (see Sugar Stages and Temperatures). Remove from heat, and add jam, rum, and lemon juice. Sprinkle mixture over the pieces of scooped-out cake, add fruit, and mix in well. Fill cake shell with this mixture. Spread a thin layer of jam on top, and replace the cut-off portion of cake. Cover with a board and weight, and chill for 6 to 8 hours. Remove loaf cake from pan; decorate with icing.

PLAIN GINGERBREAD
JEDNODUCHÝ PERNÍK LITÝ

4⅓ cups flour
¾ cup sugar
4 teaspoons single-acting
   baking powder (see
   Explanatory Notes)
8 teaspoons Gingerbread
   Spice (see below)

½ cup honey
¼ cup butter, melted
1 egg, lightly beaten
½ cup milk or black
   coffee
fine bread crumbs

Sift dry ingredients into bowl. Heat honey to lukewarm; mix the butter, egg, and milk or coffee into it. Add to flour mixture and beat into a smooth soft dough. Let stand for 1 to 2 hours. Grease a baking pan, sprinkle with bread crumbs; pour in batter. Bake in a preheated oven at 350° for 10 minutes; reduce heat to 325° and bake another 45 to 60 minutes.

BLACK-AND-WHITE CAKE
KAKAOVÝ DORT SKLÁDANÝ

LIGHT BATTER

3 egg whites
½ cup plus 1 tablespoon
   confectioners' sugar
⅓ cup flour
3 tablespoons butter,
   melted and cooled

Vanilla Cream Filling
   (see Index)

DARK BATTER

2 eggs separated
2 tablespoons sugar
1 tablespoon flour
1 tablespoon cocoa

1 teaspoon cocoa

To make Light Batter, beat egg whites until very stiff. Fold in sugar, then flour. Carefully blend in melted butter. Bake in a greased and floured 8- or 9-inch deep cake pan in a preheated 350° oven for about 45 minutes. Cool on a rack.

To make Dark Batter, beat egg whites until very stiff. Add egg yolks, 1 at a time, sprinkling each with sugar and flour mixed with cocoa; blend in gently. Bake in a greased and floured 8- or 9-inch cake pan in a preheated oven at 350° for about 30 minutes. Cool on a rack.

Split light cake into 2 layers. Spread Vanilla Cream Filling on 1 layer; top it with dark layer. Spread more cream filling on this, and top it with remaining light layer. Decorate top and sides of cake with balance of cream. Sift cocoa over top.

BISHOP'S BREAD I
BISKUPSKÝ CHLEBÍČEK

1 recipe Pound Cake batter I or II (see Index)	¼ cup sliced Blanched Almonds (see Index)
¾ cup candied fruit	fine bread crumbs

Prepare pound cake batter, using ½ cup less of flour. Stir in fruit and almonds. Grease a loaf pan and sprinkle with bread crumbs. Pour in batter, and bake in a preheated 325° oven for 30 to 45 minutes. When cake is cool, decorate with Chocolate Icing, or serve sliced with Cocoa Sauce or Vanilla Sauce (see Index).

BISHOP'S BREAD II
BISKUPSKÝ CHLEBÍČEK

1 recipe Sponge Cake batter (see Index)	⅓ cup sliced filberts
	⅓ cup chocolate chips
⅓ cup raisins	⅓ cup diced dried apricots
⅓ cup citron, cut into small strips	fine bread crumbs
	Water Icing (see Index)

Prepare cake batter. Blend into it all ingredients above. Pour into a greased 5- by 9-inch loaf pan sprinkled with bread crumbs. Bake in a preheated 325° oven for 40 to 50 minutes. When cake is cool, decorate with Water Icing.

GINGERBREAD SPICE
PERNÍKOVÉ KOŘENÍ

2 teaspoons ground
    cinnamon
2 teaspoons ground cloves
2 teaspoons ground allspice

4 teaspoons ground anise
4 teaspoons ground star
    anise
1 vanilla bean, ground

This mixture is enough for 9 cups of the flour.

This may also be purchased in ready-to-use form (see Explanatory Notes).

HONEY CAKE
JEMNÝ PERNÍK

2⅓ cups all-purpose flour
2 cups instantized flour
1 cup sugar
2 teaspoons single-acting
    baking powder (see
    Explanatory Notes)
    or ½ teaspoon
    baking soda
8 teaspoons Gingerbread
    Spice (see Index)
⅔ cup honey
¼ cup milk

2 egg yolks, lightly
    beaten
1 tablespoon rum
1 teaspoon grated lemon
    peel
1 teaspoon grated orange
    peel
½ cup raisins
½ cup chopped Blanched
    Almonds (see
    Index)
½ cup chopped walnuts
fine bread crumbs

Sift all dry ingredients into a bowl. Heat honey to lukewarm; add milk, egg yolks, rum, and peels to it. Pour into flour mixture and beat to a smooth soft dough. Mix in raisins, almonds, and walnuts. Let batter rest overnight (10 to 12 hours) in a cool, not cold, place. (If dough gets too thick, warm it up a little by placing over a pan of hot water before pouring into baking pan.) Grease a 4-sided baking sheet and sprinkle with bread crumbs. Spread dough on evenly, about 1 inch high. Bake in a preheated 325° oven for about 30 minutes. When cake is cool, decorate with Cocoa Icing

MALAKOV CAKE
DORT MALAKOV

½ cup butter	¾ cup grated
½ cup plus 2 tablespoons	Blanched
sugar	Almonds (see
3 egg yolks	Index)
	1 cup heavy cream
	40–50 (approximately)
	ladyfingers

Cream butter thoroughly with sugar and egg yolks. Add almonds, mix well. Pour in cream slowly, beating continuously. Line a spring form with waxed paper, and line the sides and bottom with ladyfingers. Fill pan with alternate layers of batter and ladyfingers, ending with ladyfingers. Cover form with waxed paper and place on it another cake pan holding a weight. Put in refrigerator overnight. Remove cake from form, and decorate with Whipped Cream.

MERINGUE CAKE
PĚNOVÝ DORT BEZÉ

5 egg whites	1 cup plus 4 teaspoons
1 cup sugar	confectioners' sugar,
½ teaspoon vanilla	sifted

Beat egg whites until stiff; beat in sugar, adding it slowly. Add vanilla; fold in confectioners' sugar. Grease two 4-sided baking sheets, line them with waxed paper, and grease again. With a pastry tube, shape meringue into two 9-inch spirals, starting from the center. Bake in a preheated 250° oven for 30 to 40 minutes. Turn off heat and open oven door about 2 inches; let cakes cool in the oven. Peel off waxed paper. Fill layers with Coffee Cream Filling or Chocolate Cream Filling (see Index).

NUT COFFEE CAKE
OŘÍŠKOVÝ KÁVOVÝ DORT

5 eggs, separated
½ cup plus 2 tablespoons
   sugar
1 tablespoon finely
   ground coffee

½ cup ground filberts
¼ cup flour
sliced Toasted Filberts
   (see Index)

Beat egg whites until stiff. Blend in egg yolks gently, 1 at a time, sprinkling each first with sugar. Mix together coffee, ground filberts, and flour, and fold lightly into egg mixture. Pour into a greased and floured spring form. Bake in a preheated 325° oven for 30 to 45 minutes. When cake is cool, fill and frost with Coffee Cream Filling (see Index), and decorate with sliced Toasted Filberts.

ECONOMY NUT CAKE
OŘÍŠKOVÝ DORT LEVNÝ

3 eggs, separated
¾ cup sugar
3 tablespoons hot water

1 cup flour
½ cup ground Toasted
   Filberts (see Index)

Beat egg yolks thoroughly with half the sugar. Add water; beat until foamy. Beat egg whites until very stiff, adding the remaining sugar gradually; mixture will be thick and glossy. Mix flour with nuts. Fold egg-yolk mixture into egg whites alternately with flour mixture. Pour batter into a greased and floured 9-inch deep cake pan; bake in a preheated 325° oven for 30 to 45 minutes. Fill with Coffee Cream Filling or Vanilla Cream Filling (see Index).

PANAMA CAKE
DORT PANAMA

6 eggs, separated
¾ cup sugar
1½ ounces (squares)
chocolate, melted

1 cup grated almonds
fine bread crumbs

Beat egg yolks with sugar until foamy; add chocolate, blend well. Fold in stiffly beaten egg whites alternately with almonds. Pour into a greased spring form sprinkled with bread crumbs. Bake in a preheated oven at 325° for 40 to 50 minutes. When cake is cool, decorate with Cocoa Cream Filling (see Index).

POPPY SEED CAKE
MAKOVEC BRAMBOROVÝ

1 egg yolk
¾ cup sugar
4 tablespoons milk
2 (scant ½ pound) cold
boiled potatoes,
grated
¼ cup farina
¾ cup ground poppy seed
4 teaspoons single-acting
baking powder (see
Explanatory Notes)

¼ teaspoon cinnamon
pinch of ground cloves
½ teaspoon ground lemon
peel
½ teaspoon vanilla
2 egg whites, stiffly
beaten
fine bread crumbs
jam

Beat egg yolk, sugar, and milk together until creamy. Add potatoes, farina, and poppy seeds mixed with baking powder, cinnamon, and cloves. Blend in lemon peel and vanilla. Fold in egg whites. Grease a spring form and sprinkle with bread crumbs; pour in batter. Bake in a preheated 350° oven for 40 to 50 minutes. When cake is cool, spread jam on top, and decorate with Cocoa or Rum Icing.

FRUIT CAKE
BUBLANINA

1 recipe Sponge Cake
batter (see Index)
½–1 pound fresh fruit
(cherries, blueber-
ries, raspberries,
or strawberries)

¼ cup (approximately)
instantized flour
fine bread crumbs
confectioners' sugar

Grease a 4-sided baking sheet and sprinkle with bread crumbs. Pour in batter, and spread evenly in a layer about 1 to 1½ inches thick. Dust fruit with flour, and arrange on top of batter. Bake in a preheated 325° oven for 20 to 30 minutes. Cool. To serve, cut into squares and sprinkle with sugar.

SPECIAL CROWN CAKE
JEMNÁ BÁBOVKA

1 cup butter
1¼ cups sugar
5 eggs, separated
2¼ cups instantized flour
1 cup milk
2 teaspoons single-acting
baking powder (see
Explanatory Notes)

½ teaspoon grated lemon
peel
1 teaspoon vanilla
⅓ cup chocolate pieces,
melted
2 tablespoons (approxi-
mately) oil for pan

Cream butter and sugar, add egg yolks, beat until light and creamy. Mix in flour and milk alternately by spoonfuls. Add the baking powder mixed into the last ½ cup flour. Blend in lemon peel and vanilla. Fold in stiffly beaten egg whites. Pour half the batter into another bowl and add the chocolate to it. Brush a fluted tube pan with oil, and pour in batter in four alternating light and dark layers. Cut through batter with a spoon to get a marbled effect. Bake in a preheated 350° oven for 60 to 75 minutes. Cool in pan for 15 minutes, then turn cake out onto a wire rack. Sprinkle with Vanilla Sugar (see Index) when cool.

PUNCH CAKE
PUNČOVÝ DORT

CAKE	PUNCH
6 eggs, separated	½ cup sugar
½ cup sugar	½ cup water
1 teaspoon vanilla	1 lemon, juice only
1 cup flour	⅓ cup rum
1 tablespoon cocoa	2 tablespoons jam
red food coloring	

4 tablespoons currant or
    apricot jam

To make cake, beat egg whites until very stiff. Blend in egg yolks, 1 at a time, sprinkling each with sugar before blending. Add vanilla. Fold in flour. Fill a greased and floured spring form half full; divide remaining batter among 3 bowls. Add cocoa to one, and a few drops of coloring to the second; leave the third as is. Grease and flour a 4-sided baking sheet. Cut 2 pieces of cardboard the width of the sheet. Pour white batter onto one-third of the sheet and block it with cardboard; pour on cocoa batter, block with cardboard; pour colored batter onto last section. Put spring form and baking sheet into a preheated oven and bake at 350° for 20 to 30 minutes. Cool.

To prepare punch, cook sugar and water until sirupy; remove from heat, add remaining ingredients.

To finish, split round cake into 2 layers. Spread the cut side of each with jam, and sprinkle 1 tablespoon of the punch over it. Cut sheet cake into 1-inch cubes, mix colors together; sprinkle them with punch. Line a spring form with waxed paper. Place 1 round layer, cut side up, on the bottom; spread a layer of punch-soaked cubes over it, and cover with the second round layer, placed cut side down. Cover the whole with waxed paper and place another cake pan on it. Put a weight on top. Let cake stand overnight in the refrigerator. Next day, remove from form, spread very thinly with jam, and pour on Rum or Fondant Icing (see Index).

RUSKS
SUCHÁRKY

1 recipe Sponge Cake
    batter (see Index)
½ cup sliced Blanched
    Almonds (see Index)

½ cup butter, melted
Vanilla Sugar (see
    Index)

Prepare batter, fold almonds in it. Pour into 2 greased and floured 5- by 9-inch loaf pans. Bake in a preheated 350° oven for 20 to 30 minutes. Cool, then cut into ½-inch-thick slices. Brush with butter on both sides. Put on a baking sheet and bake for 10 to 20 minutes, turning once. Roll in Vanilla Sugar while hot.

SACHER CAKE
SACHRŮV DORT

5 tablespoons butter
½ cup plus 1 tablespoon
    sugar
6 eggs, separated

2 ounces (squares)
    chocolate, melted
¾ cup flour
⅓ cup grated almonds
2 tablespoons apricot jam

Cream butter with sugar and egg yolks until foamy. Add chocolate. Fold in stiffly beaten egg whites, then fold in flour mixed with almonds. Pour into a greased and floured spring form. Bake in a preheated 350° oven for 45 to 60 minutes. When cake is cool, spread with a very thin layer of jam, and pour over it Chocolate or Cocoa Icing (see Index). Decorate with Whipped Cream (see Index).

SADDLE CAKE
SRNČÍ HŘBET

5 eggs, separated	1 cup grated almonds
¾ cup sugar	fine bread crumbs
3 ounces (squares)	1 tablespoon apricot jam
chocolate, melted	Chocolate or Cocoa
pinch of cinnamon	Icing (see Index)
½ cup bread crumbs	1–2 tablespoons slivered
2 tablespoons white wine	almonds

Beat egg yolks and sugar until foamy. Add chocolate, cinnamon, and bread crumbs sprinkled with wine. Fold in stiffly beaten egg whites, then fold in grated almonds. Grease a fluted loaf pan and sprinkle with fine bread crumbs. Pour in batter, and bake in a preheated 350° oven for 30 to 40 minutes. Cool. Spread a very thin layer of jam on cake; pour on icing. Stick in slivered almonds, porcupine style.

SADDLE CAKE, ECONOMY STYLE
SRNČÍ HŘBET LEVNÝ

6 tablespoons butter	2 teaspoons single-acting
¾ cup sugar	baking powder (see
2 eggs, separated	Explanatory Notes)
2 tablespoons cocoa	1 tablespoon jam
½ cup milk	Cocoa Icing (see
1⅔ cups flour	Index)
	1 tablespoon slivered
	almonds

Cream butter thoroughly with sugar and egg yolks. Mix in cocoa. Sift flour with baking powder; add to creamed mixture alternately with milk. Fold in stiffly beaten egg whites. Grease and flour a large fluted loaf pan; pour in batter. Bake in a preheated 300° oven for about 30 minutes. Finish like Saddle Cake (above).

SPONGE CAKE
PIŠKOT ŠLEHANÝ

4 eggs, separated
¾ cup sugar
1 cup flour
½ teaspoon lemon juice

½ teaspoon grated lemon peel
fine bread crumbs

Beat egg whites to soft peaks. Add ⅓ cup sugar, beat until whites are very stiff and glossy. Fold in egg yolks, 1 at a time, sprinkling each before blending with part of the remaining sugar and flour. Gently blend in lemon juice and peel. Grease a spring form and sprinkle with bread crumbs; pour in batter. Bake in a preheated 325° oven for 30 to 45 minutes. Cool cake for 15 minutes, then remove from pan.

QUICK SPONGE CAKE
PIŠKOTOVÝ DORT BEZ VÁŽENÍ

4 eggs, separated
4 tablespoons sugar
4 tablespoons flour

Beat egg whites until very stiff. Blend in egg yolks, 1 at a time, sprinkling each with sugar before adding it. Sprinkle batter with flour; fold in carefully. Pour into a greased and floured 8- or 9-inch deep cake pan. Bake in a preheated 325° oven for 30 to 40 minutes. When cake is cool, split it into 2 layers. Fill and decorate with Butter Cream Filling of your choice.

DRY CAKE CRUMBS
PŘÍPRAVA SLADKÝCH DROBTŮ

Prepare Sponge Cake (see Index). Bake on a greased and floured baking sheet in a preheated 325° oven for about 20 minutes. Cut in pieces and dry in the oven. Grate and sift. Store in an airtight jar.

WALNUT CAKE
DORT OŘECHOVÝ

6 eggs, separated
½ cup sugar
⅔ cup ground walnuts

½ cup flour
⅔ cup fine bread crumbs

Beat egg whites until very stiff. Carefully blend in egg yolks, 1 at a time, sprinkling each with sugar before blending. Mix nuts, flour, and bread crumbs together; fold lightly into batter. Pour into a greased and floured spring form. Bake in a preheated 325° oven for 45 to 60 minutes. Cover with Whipped Cream, Vanilla Cream Filling, or Coffee Cream Filling.

WALNUT CAKE WITH EGG WHITES
OŘECHOVÝ DORT Z BÍLKU

1 cup ground almonds
9 egg whites
½ cup, plus 2 tablespoons
    sugar

½ teaspoon vanilla
⅓ cup instantized flour

Mix nuts with 3 egg whites, sugar, and vanilla; blend well. Beat the remaining egg whites stiffly; fold in. Fold flour into mixture. Grease and flour a 4-sided baking sheet and a spring form. Fill a pastry tube with part of the batter and press 12 small rosettes onto the baking sheet. Pour the remaining batter into the spring form. Bake cake and rosettes in a preheated 275° oven for 20 to 30 minutes. When cake is cool, split it into 2 layers. Fill and decorate with Whipped Cream or Vanilla Cream Filling (see Index). Decorate border of cake with rosettes.

PASTRIES

INDIANS
INDIÁNKY

3 egg yolks
3 tablespoons sugar
¾ cup flour
4 egg whites

Whipped Cream or Cooked
Meringue Filling (see
Index)
Cocoa Icing (see Index)

Beat egg yolks with 1 tablespoon sugar and flour. Beat egg whites until stiff, then slowly add the remaining sugar, beating constantly. Fold in egg-yolk mixture. Grease and flour a baking sheet, and press dough through a plain pastry tube onto it to form 2-inch-wide mounds. Bake in a preheated 325° oven for 15 to 20 minutes. Pour icing over half the mounds. Place the rest in fluted paper cups, rounded side down. Fill with Whipped Cream or Cooked Meringue Filling, and top each with an iced mound.

PASTRY POTATOES
BRAMBŮRKY

baked mounds for Indians
(see Index)
Cocoa Butter Cream Icing
(see Index)
Almond Paste (see Index)

1 egg white, lightly
beaten
½ cup cocoa
¼ cup sugar

Scoop out baked mounds on flat side and fill with butter cream; put together in pairs. Roll out Almond Paste ⅛ inch thick on a sugared board and cut into squares large enough to fit as a wrap around paired mounds. Brush edges of Almond Paste with egg white and press together to seal. Roll "potatoes" in cocoa mixed with sugar; place in fluted paper cups to serve. With a sharp knife make "cracks" and "eyes" in the "potatoes."

PASTRY FRUIT
ZÁKUSKY VE TVARU OVOCE

1 recipe dough for Indians
  (see Index)
Vanilla Butter Cream
  Icing (see Index)
Almond Paste (see
  Index)

1 egg white, lightly beaten
food colors
Cocoa Icing (see Index—
  optional)

Prepare dough for Indians, but press batter through a plain pastry tube into pairs of fruit shapes (pears, apples, fresh prunes, apricots, peaches). Bake like Indians. Scoop out each "fruit" piece on the flat side, fill with butter cream; put together in pairs. Roll out Almond Paste on a sugared board to ⅛ inch thickness; cut into pieces large enough to wrap around "fruit." Brush edges with egg white; press together to seal. Let "fruit" dry, then paint with food color to resemble real fruit. Use real stems, or dip toothpicks in Cocoa Icing to make stems. Place in fluted paper cups to serve.

CHOCOLATE BALLS
ČOKOLÁDOVÉ KOULE

baked mounds for Indians
  (see Index)

Butter Cream Icing (see
  Index)
1 cup chocolate, grated

Scoop out mounds and fill with butter cream. Put together in pairs to form balls. Spread icing over balls, then roll in chocolate. Place in fluted paper cups to serve.

NUT BALLS
OŘECHOVÉ KOULE

Prepare like Chocolate Balls (above), but roll balls in finely chopped walnuts or Toasted Filberts (see Index) instead of chocolate.

LINZ TARTS
LINECKÉ KOŠÍČKY

CRUST

1 recipe for dough for
De Luxe Linz Pastry
(see Index)

FILLING

6 tablespoons butter
½ cup sugar
3 eggs, separated
½ teaspoon vanilla
1 teaspoon grated lemon
peel
¾ cup Dry Cake Crumbs
(see Index)
½ cup ground almonds or
other nuts
1 egg, lightly beaten (for
brushing tarts)

Prepare dough; press into tart forms.

To prepare filling, cream butter thoroughly with sugar and egg yolks. Add vanilla and lemon peel. Fold in stiffly beaten egg whites and cake crumbs mixed with nuts. Pour into unbaked tart shells. Shape leftover dough into thin rolls; cut to fit across tarts. Brush with egg. Put on a baking sheet; bake in a preheated 350° oven for 20 to 30 minutes.

CRISP TARTLETS
KŘEHKÉ MALÉ DORTÍČKY

CRUST	FILLING
2 cups flour	2 egg yolks or 1 egg
6 tablespoons sugar	½ cup plus 1 tablespoon
1 tablespoon cocoa	sugar
¼ cup ground almonds	2 tablespoons currant
¾ cup butter	or cherry jam
1 egg yolk	½–¾ cup ground
1 teaspoon vanilla	Toasted Filberts
	(see Index)

Chocolate or Fondant Icing (see Index)

Mix together dry ingredients for tartlets. Work in butter and egg yolk to form a dough. Roll out on lightly floured board to ¼ inch thickness; cut into 3-inch circles. Place on a baking sheet and bake in a preheated 350° oven for 10 to 20 minutes.

To prepare filling, beat egg yolks or egg with sugar, add jam and vanilla; beat until foamy. Blend in filberts. Put tartlets together in pairs with filling between them. Pour icing on top.

MERINGUE PASTRY
PĚNOVÉ BEZÉ

Meringue Cake batter
  (see Index)
Whipped Cream, Parisian
  Cream, or Coffee Cream
  Filling (see Index)

Press batter into 2½-inch-wide mound onto a greased baking sheet lined with waxed paper. Bake in a preheated 250° oven for 30 to 45 minutes or until dry. Put together in pairs filled with cream; place in fluted paper cups to serve.

MOCHA TARTLETS
MOKKA PLACIČKY

5 egg whites
¾ cup plus 2 tablespoons sugar
¾ cup ground nuts
½ cup instantized flour

1½ tablespoons melted butter, cooled
Butter Cream or Parisian Cream (see Index)
Cocoa Icing (see Index)

Beat egg whites until stiff. Fold in sugar mixed with nuts and flour. Slowly pour in melted butter; mix lightly. Press through a pastry tube onto a greased baking sheet (shape into ovals 3½ by 2 inches). Bake in a preheated 300° oven for 10 to 20 minutes. Cool. Put together in pairs filled with cream. Decorate with icing pressed through a decorating tube into a lattice design.

YOLK FLOWER BOXES
ŽLOUTKOVÉ RAKVIČKY

"BOXES" PASTRY

2⅓ cups confectioners' sugar
5 egg yolks
1 egg
1 tablespoon instantized flour
1 teaspoon vanilla

FILLING

Whipped Cream or Mock Whipped Cream (see Index)

Beat all ingredients for "boxes" in an electric mixer or with a wire whisk until thick and foamy (about 45 minutes). Prepare the tiny loaf pans used for these (or éclair molds) by brushing with melted butter and sprinkling with flour; fill two-thirds full with batter. Bake in a preheated 375° oven for

10 minutes or until "boxes" are puffed up, then reduce heat to 325° and bake 10 to 15 minutes longer. Cool in pans. With the point of a knife, make small openings in both ends of pastry. Force in whipped cream with a pastry tube, and decorate top with a line of cream.

MERINGUE CRESCENTS WITH NUTS
OŘÍŠKOVÉ PĚNOVÉ ROHLÍČKY

4 egg whites
1 cup superfine sugar

1 cup ground filberts or almonds

Beat egg whites and sugar in a double boiler until thick. Place by spoonfuls on a board sprinkled with the nuts. Roll in nuts and shape into crescents. Bake on a greased baking sheet in a preheated 200° oven until crisp (about 40 to 50 minutes).

HAZELNUT ARCHES
OŘÍŠKOVÉ OBLOUČKY

3 egg whites
1⅓ cups superfine sugar
2 cups ground hazelnuts

3–4 White Wafer Sheets, 8 by 11 inches (see Explanatory Notes)

Beat egg whites until stiff. Fold in sugar mixed with nuts. Spread about ¼ inch thick over wafer sheets. Cut through paper into strips ¾ inch wide by 4 inches long. Grease the rounded outside bottom of a fluted loaf pan. Lay strips on top to shape them into arches. Bake in a preheated 250° oven until arches are crisp on top (15 to 30 minutes).

LATTICE PIE
KOLÁČ MŘÍŽKOVÝ

1 recipe Plain Linz Pastry
    (see Index)
1 cup jam or 1–2 cups
    Poppy Seed, Cheese,
    Nut, or Apple Filling
    (see Index)

1 egg white, lightly
    beaten

Prepare pastry. Roll out two-thirds of dough on lightly floured board, and use it to line bottom of a large spring form. Roll out the remaining dough; from it cut a 1-inch strip and use it to line sides of the form. Spread dough with jam or filling. Cut ½-inch-wide strips from balance of dough with a pastry wheel. Lay across filling in a diagonal lattice pattern. (Or cut out small cookie shapes from dough and use instead of lattice to top filling.) Brush top with egg white. Bake pie in a preheated 350° oven for 45 to 60 minutes. Remove from pan, cool on a wire rack. Serves 6 to 8.

VIENNESE PATIENCE
PASIÁNS

1 cup plus 6 tablespoons
    sugar
1 cup black coffee

4 egg whites
2 cups flour

Add sugar to coffee and cook to thread stage (see Sugar Stages and Temperatures). Blend into stiffly beaten egg whites. Fold in flour. Cool. Lightly grease a baking sheet. Press dough through a plain pastry tube onto the baking sheet and form into the usual patience shapes (hearts, clubs, diamonds, and spades), as well as into numbers and letters of the alphabet. Make the shapes 2 to 3 inches high. Let stand in a warm place for 1 to 2 hours, then bake in a preheated 200° oven until dry.

CELESTIAL FAVORS
BOŽÍ MILOSTI

I. Economy Dough

2 cups instantized flour
2 tablespoons sugar
  pinch of salt
2 tablespoons butter
1 egg yolk
2 tablespoons rum

½ teaspoon grated
  lemon peel
1 egg white, slightly
  beaten
1–2 cups shortening
  (for frying)
  Vanilla Sugar (see
  Index)

Sift dry ingredients onto a pastry board. Crumble in butter, and mix in egg yolk, rum, and grated lemon peel. Knead until smooth and shiny. Flour board lightly and roll dough out ⅛ inch thick. Cut with a pastry wheel into squares, diamonds, or triangles. Or cut stars in 2 sizes; brush the larger with egg white, place the smaller star on top, and join by pressing in the center with your finger. Prick pastry shapes with a fork and fry in hot shortening for about 3 minutes on each side. Drain on absorbent paper, and dust with Vanilla Sugar.

II. Fine Dough

2 cups instantized flour
1 teaspoon butter
2 egg yolks
1 egg
2 tablespoons rum
4 teaspoons lemon juice

½ teaspoon grated
  lemon peel
1 egg white, slightly
  beaten
1–2 cups shortening
  (for frying)
  Vanilla Sugar (see
  Index)

Prepare like Celestial Favors made with Economy Dough (above).

LINZ PASTRY
LINECKÉ TĚSTO

I. Plain Linz Pastry

2½ cups flour
½ cup sugar
½ cup butter
1 egg

1–2 tablespoons milk
½ teaspoon grated
lemon peel
½ teaspoon vanilla

Sift dry ingredients onto a pastry board; cut in butter. Make a well in the center and add the remaining ingredients. Mix with a fork, then knead. Chill before using.

II. De Luxe Linz Pastry

2¾ cups flour
⅓ cup sugar
1 cup butter
2 egg yolks

½ teaspoon grated lemon
peel
½ teaspoon vanilla

Prepare like Plain Linz Pastry (above).

DATE KISSES
DATLOVÉ PUSINKY

3 egg whites
¾ cup superfine sugar
⅔ cup dates, pitted and
cut into strips

¾ cup sliced Blanched
Almonds (see Index)

Beat egg whites until stiff. Fold in sugar, dates, and almonds. Drop in small mounds from a teaspoon onto a greased baking sheet. Bake in a preheated 200° oven until crisp (about 1 hour).

POPPY SEED PIE

KOLÁČ S MAKOVOU NÁDIVKOU

CRUST

1 recipe De Luxe Linz
   Pastry
1–2 cups Poppy Seed
   Filling (see Index)

MERINGUE

5 egg whites
¾ cup superfine sugar

Prepare pastry. Roll out dough on a lightly floured board and line bottom and sides of a large spring form with it. Spread filling on top. Bake in a preheated 350° oven for about 30 minutes.

To make meringue, beat egg whites; add sugar gradually, beating continuously until whites are very stiff and glossy. Spread meringue over pie, and return to oven. Bake for 15 to 20 minutes longer. Remove pie from pan and cool on wire rack. Serves 6 to 8.

JELLIED FRUIT TARTS

KOŠÍČKY

Proceed as for Jellied Fruit Pie (below), but use individual tart pans instead of a spring form to prepare tart shells. Bake shells in a preheated 400° oven for 15 to 20 minutes.

JELLIED FRUIT PIE
KOLÁČ OVOCNÝ "POD SKLEM"

CRUST

1 recipe De Luxe Linz
   Pastry (see Index)
1 egg, lightly beaten
2 tablespoons jam
2–3 cups fruit (fresh, or
   drained canned)

FILLING

2 envelopes gelatin
1½ cups cold water
¾ cup sugar
1 teaspoon lemon juice

Prepare dough. Roll out two-thirds on a lightly floured board, and line bottom of a large spring form with it. Roll out the remaining dough, and from it cut 2-inch strips and use to line sides of the form. Brush dough with egg white, and bake in a preheated 350° oven for 20 to 30 minutes. Remove crust from pan; cool. Then brush inside with jam, and arrange fruit on top.

To prepare filling, soak gelatin in ½ cup water. Meanwhile, bring sugar, 1 cup water, and lemon juice to a boil. Add gelatin, stirring constantly to dissolve, but do not let mixture boil. Place pan in a bowl of cold water, and continue to stir until thickened. Pour over fruit. Chill. Serves 6.

QUICK CRUMB PIE
DROBENKOVÝ KOLÁČ RYCHLÝ

2¼ cups instantized flour
½ teaspoon baking
   powder
½ cup sugar
½ cup butter
1 egg, lightly beaten
½ teaspoon vanilla

½ teaspoon grated lemon
   peel
1 pound apples, pared
   and sliced
¼ cup sugar
¼ cup butter, melted
1 tablespoon sugar (for
   top)

Mix together dry ingredients, and rub in butter to form

crumbs. Mix in egg, vanilla, and lemon peel. Crumble again with your fingers. Put half the crumbs in a buttered and floured cake pan. Spread on apples, sprinkle with the ¼ cup sugar and half the melted butter. Cover with the remaining crumbs, and sprinkle with the tablespoon sugar and the rest of butter. Bake in a preheated 400° oven for 30 to 45 minutes. Serves 4 to 6.

WALNUT PIE

KOLÁČ OŘECHOVÝ

CRUST	FILLING
1 recipe De Luxe Linz Pastry (see Index) 1 egg white, lightly beaten 4 teaspoons Crystal Sugar (see Explanatory Notes)	¾ cup sugar 3 eggs, separated ½ teaspoon grated lemon peel ½ teaspoon vanilla 1⅓ cups ground walnuts

Prepare pastry. Roll out two-thirds of dough on lightly floured board and line bottom of a large spring form with it. Roll out remaining dough; cut a 1½-inch strip from it, and use to line sides of the form.

To prepare filling, beat sugar and egg yolks together until foamy. Add lemon peel, vanilla, and walnuts, and blend. Fold in stiffly beaten egg whites.

Spread filling in pan and cover with rest of dough. Brush with egg white and sprinkle with Crystal Sugar. Bake in a preheated 350° oven for 45 to 60 minutes; remove from pan and cool on a wire rack.

STRETCHED STRUDEL DOUGH
ZÁVIN TAŽENÝ

2⅔ cups flour	½ cup lukewarm water
pinch of salt	½ teaspoon vinegar
1 egg, lightly beaten	1 tablespoon lard, melted

Sift flour onto a pastry board and make a well in the center. Mix together salt, egg, water, vinegar, and lard, and add gradually to flour, stirring with a fork until flour is completely moistened. Knead dough until smooth and elastic. Shape into a ball, and let it rest, covered with a warm, inverted bowl, on lightly floured board for 30 minutes.

Cover a table with a clean cloth and sprinkle with flour. Place dough in the center, dust with flour, and roll out ⅛ inch thick. Slide hands under dough, and with the backs of your clenched fists, start stretching it, working from center in all directions, and being careful not to tear it. When center of dough becomes paper thin, concentrate the stretching closer to dough edges. Stretched dough should finally be as thin as tissue paper. Fill as directed in one of the following recipes.

I. Apple Strudel
Jablkový závin

1 recipe Stretched Strudel Dough (above)	3 tablespoons butter
	½ cup sugar
½ cup butter, melted	1 teaspoon cinnamon
2 pounds apples, pared and sliced	⅓ cup raisins
	confectioners' sugar
1 cup bread crumbs	

Brush prepared dough generously with part of the melted butter and sprinkle with bread crumbs browned in the 3 tablespoons butter. Spread apples evenly over dough; sprinkle with sugar mixed with cinnamon, raisins, and more melted butter. Grasp cloth holding dough on one side with both

hands. Lift slowly, and start rolling up dough, brushing under-
side with butter as you roll. Roll strudel from the cloth onto
a greased baking sheet. Brush top with butter and bake in a
350° oven for about 30 minutes. Dust with confectioners'
sugar. Slice to serve.

II. Cherry Strudel
Třešňovy závin

1 recipe Stretched Strudel	2 pounds sour (or
Dough (above)	sweet) cherries,
½ cup butter, melted	pitted
1 cup bread crumbs	½–1 cup sugar
3 tablespoons butter	confectioners' sugar

Follow instructions for making Apple Strudel (above). The
amount of sugar used will depend on tartness of the cherries.

III. Cabbage Strudel
Zelný závin

1 recipe Stretched Strudel	salt to taste
Dough (above)	pepper to taste
½ cup butter, melted	½ cup heavy cream
4 cups (1 pound)	½–1 cup chopped cooked
shredded cabbage	ham
½ cup water	confectioners' sugar
¼ cup shortening, melted	(optional)

Cook cabbage in water for 10 minutes. Drain. Add to shortening; cook until all liquid evaporates. Mix in salt, pepper,
cream, and ham. Cool. Proceed as for Apple Strudel (above),
but do not add sugar.

Instead of this filling, you may use a sweet cabbage filling
(see Cabbage Rolls in Index). Sprinkle with confectioners'
sugar.

ROLLED-OUT STRUDEL
ZÁVIN VYVALOVANÝ

DOUGH
1⅓ cups flour
pinch of salt
1 teaspoon shortening,
    melted
1 egg
1 egg yolk
½ cup water
confectioners' sugar

FILLING
1 pound apples
¼ cup sugar
½ teaspoon cinnamon
½ cup (approximately)
    butter, melted
½ cup bread crumbs

To make dough, sift flour, mix together salt, shortening, lightly beaten eggs, and water, and add to flour. Work into a smooth dough. Divide into 4 pieces. Roll out each piece on a lightly floured board into a very thin sheet.

To prepare filling, pare and slice apples, spread on sheets of dough, sprinkle with cinnamon, sugar, ⅓ cup melted butter, and bread crumbs. Roll up individual strudels. Lay on a well-greased baking pan, and brush with butter. Bake in a 350° oven for 20 to 30 minutes. Dust with sugar. Slice to serve.

YOLK CREAM WREATHS
ŽLOUTKOVÉ VĚNEČKY

1 recipe Cream Puffs dough
    (see Index)
1 recipe Yolk Pastry Cream
    (see Index)

confectioners' sugar

Prepare dough, and force through a pastry bag onto a greased baking sheet into 3-inch rings. Bake in a preheated 450° oven for 10 minutes. Reduce heat to 350° and bake 10 to 20 minutes longer. When wreaths are cool, cut off top and fill with cream. Replace top; dust with sugar.

FRENCH PASTRIES
ŘEZY

1 recipe Pound Cake I or
    II
jam, frosting, icing,
    chopped nuts,
    candied cherries, or
    coconut, etc.

red food coloring
    (optional)
¼ cup cocoa (optional)
    fine bread crumbs

Prepare batter; spread on a greased, 4-sided pan sprinkled with bread crumbs to a depth of about ¾ inch. Bake in a preheated 300° oven for 10 to 20 minutes. When cake is cool, cut into various shapes, 2 to 3 inches in diameter, making 2 of each shape. Spread half the pieces with jam, frosting, or any other desired filling, then cover each shape with its twin, and decorate with more frosting or icing, chopped nuts, candied cherries, or coconut, etc.

Mix a few drops of food coloring into batter to make pastries more colorful, or add cocoa to it before baking.

CREAM PUFFS
ODPALOVANÉ TĚSTO

1 cup water
    pinch of salt
6 tablespoons butter

1¼ cups instantized flour
4 eggs

Bring, water, salt, and butter to a rolling boil. Add flour all at once. Beat quickly with a wooden spoon until mixture leaves sides of pan and forms a smooth ball. Remove from heat, and beat in eggs, one at a time. Continue beating until mixture is thick and smooth. Drop by tablespoonfuls 2 inches apart on a lightly greased baking sheet. Bake in a preheated 450° oven for 10 minutes; reduce heat to 350° and bake 5 to 20 minutes longer, depending on size. Fill with Yolk Pastry Cream or Whipped Cream (see Index).

COFFEE ÉCLAIRS
KÁVOVÉ BANÁNY

1 recipe Cream Puffs dough
(see Index)
1 recipe Coffee Cream
Filling (see Index)

1 recipe Coffee Icing (see
Index)

Prepare dough. Force through a pastry bag into 1-by-4½-inch oblongs onto a greased baking sheet. Bake in a preheated 450° oven for 10 minutes. Reduce heat to 350°, and bake 10 to 20 minutes longer. When éclairs are cool, cut a small opening in each at 1 end, and, using a pastry bag, force cream filling into it. Spread icing over top.

PUFF PASTE
LÍSTKOVE TĚSTO

BUTTER DOUGH

1 cup plus 2 tablespoons
butter
½ cup flour

STRUDEL DOUGH

1¾ cups flour
pinch of salt
1 egg yolk
6 tablespoons water
1 tablespoon vinegar or
lemon juice

To make Butter Dough, cut butter into flour. Work into a dough. Shape into a 5-inch-square patty, and chill.

To make Strudel Dough, sift flour onto board; make a well in center. Mix together remaining ingredients and pour into the well. Work with a fork until all flour adheres, then knead into a smooth, medium-firm dough. Let stand for 30 minutes. Flour board lightly, roll out dough to an 8-inch square. Lay Butter Dough over center of Strudel Dough and fold Strudel Dough over it (like an envelope). Press doughs lightly together; turn over. Roll out to a rectangle. Fold lower third up over center third, then fold remaining third down over first third, brushing off loose flour as you fold. Fold in thirds again. Wrap dough in a damp cloth and chill in refrigerator for an hour. Roll out and fold (as above) into thirds twice more. Wrap and chill for another 20 minutes. Dough is now ready for use in any of the following recipes.

PUFF STRUDEL
LÍSTKOVÝ ZÁVIN

1 recipe Puff Paste dough (above) 2–3 cups pared and coarsely grated apples	½ cup sugar Cheese Filling (see Index) 1 egg, beaten

Prepare dough. Roll out on a lightly floured board into 2 rectangles about ⅜ inch thick. Spread apples on 1, and sprinkle with sugar. Roll up, and seal ends. Spread cheese filling on the other rectangle; roll up, and seal ends. Brush both rolls with egg. Place on a baking sheet, and bake in a preheated 450° oven for 7 minutes; reduce heat to 400° and bake 15 to 25 minutes longer.

PASTRY CREAM STRIPS
ŘEZY ŽLOUTKOVÉ

1 recipe Puff Paste dough (see Index) Yolk Pastry Cream (see Index)	½ cup jam icing (see Index)

Prepare dough. Roll out about ⅜ inch thick on lightly floured board. Cut into 4-inch strips the length of a baking sheet. Prick with fork. Bake in a preheated 450° oven for about 10 minutes. Cool. Cover half the strips with pastry cream. Spread jam on the remaining strips, drizzle icing over them, then cut them in half, and lay them on top of cream-filled strips. Cut through bottom layer so those strips are same length as the ones on top.

CREAM ROLLS
KREMROLE

1 recipe Puff Paste dough (see Index)	Meringue Filling or Whipped Cream
1 egg, beaten	(see Index) confectioners' sugar

Prepare dough. Roll out on a lightly floured board to ⅜-inch thickness. Cut into strips 6 by 1½ inches. Wind around cream roll tubes, starting at narrower end. Press dough firmly onto tubes to start, and roll tubes to wind strips, overlapping them about ¼ inch. Do not stretch dough. When each tube is completely encased in dough, press end of strip to it, and place, that side down, on a baking sheet. Brush tops of rolls with egg. Bake in a preheated 450° oven for 10 to 15 minutes. Remove rolls from tubes with a light twist, and, when they are cool, fill with Meringue Filling or Whipped Cream forced from a pastry bag into each end. Sprinkle with sugar.

CARAMEL PATTIES
KRACHLE

1 recipe Puff Paste dough (see Index)	1 egg, beaten
1—2 cups Crystal Sugar (see Explanatory Notes)	

Prepare dough. Roll out on lightly floured board to ½-inch thickness; cut into 1-inch-square pieces. Sprinkle Crystal Sugar on board. Roll out each piece of dough on sugared surface to ¼-inch thickness. Lay pieces, sugared side up, on a baking sheet, brush with egg, and sprinkle generously with more sugar. Bake in a preheated 450° oven for 10 or 15 minutes. The crystal sugar should melt and form a thin, caramel-flavored top crust.

These patties may also be made from leftover scraps of dough.

PATTY SHELLS
PAŠTIČKY

1 recipe Puff Paste dough
  (see Index)
1 egg white, beaten

Prepare dough. Roll out on lightly floured board to ¼-inch thickness. Cut into 3-inch rounds, then, with a 2-inch cutter, remove centers from two-thirds of these, leaving ½-inch rims. Brush edges of the solid 3-inch rounds with egg white, lay a ring on top of each, brush that with egg white, and cover with a second ring. Prick rings and bases with a fork, and brush tops with egg white. Transfer shells to a baking sheet that has been rinsed with cold water and drained. Bake in a preheated 450° oven for 8 minutes; reduce heat to 350° and bake 10 to 20 minutes longer. Bake the 2-inch rounds on a separate sheet for use as covers for the filled shells or for use as hors d'oeuvre bases.

PISCHINGER TORTE
OPLATKOVÝ DORT

½ cup butter
½ cup sugar
1 egg yolk
2 tablespoons cocoa
½ cup ground Toasted
  Filberts (see Index)

5 Sugar Wafer Sheets (see
  Explanatory Notes)
Cocoa or Chocolate
  Icing (see Index)

Cream butter with sugar and egg yolk until foamy. Add cocoa and filberts. Spread filling on four of the wafers and place them one on top of the other; cover with the last wafer. Place a wooden board with weight over all, and refrigerate for 6 to 8 hours. Decorate with icing.

BRNO TORTE
DORT BRNĚNSKÝ

BATTER I	BATTER II
5 eggs, separated	7 egg whites
¾ cup sugar	1 cup sugar
1 ounce (square) chocolate, melted	5 egg yolks
	1 cup flour
2 tablespoons ground filberts	**FILLING**
⅓ cup fine bread crumbs	¾ cup butter
¾ cup flour	½ cup sugar
	1 egg yolk

To make Batter I, beat egg yolks with sugar until foamy. Blend in chocolate. Fold in stiffly beaten egg whites, then filberts mixed with bread crumbs and flour. Pour into a greased and floured spring form. Bake in a preheated 325° oven for 40 minutes. Cool.

To make Batter II, beat egg whites until stiff. Carefully blend in egg yolks, 1 at a time, sprinkling with sugar before each addition; then fold in flour. Grease and flour a 4-sided baking sheet; spread batter on it to ½-inch thickness. Bake in a preheated oven for about 20 minutes. Cool.

To make filling, cream butter thoroughly with sugar and egg yolk.

Split spring-form cake into 2 layers, and spread the cut sides with part of the filling. Spread the remaining filling over the sheet cake, and cut it into 1-inch strips. Starting at center of 1 filled round layer, place strips vertically in a continuous spiral pattern over the whole cake. Cover this with the second round layer, placing the cut and filled side down. Decorate torte with White Icing or Cocoa Icing. When cake is cut into wedges for serving, it will have a handsome design between the layers.

"MIRACLE" TORTE
LEVNÝ DORT "ZÁZRAK"

TORTE	FILLING
1 tablespoon honey	2 cups milk
½ cup sugar	⅓ cup potato starch
2½ tablespoons butter	½ cup sugar
1 teaspoon vanilla	¼ cup butter
1 egg	1 tablespoon cocoa
1 teaspoon baking soda	¼ cup chopped nuts
2 cups flour	

To make torte, put honey, sugar, butter, vanilla, and egg into top of double boiler. Beat with a wire whisk over medium heat until foamy. Add soda; beat in well. Remove from heat. Blend in flour. Turn out on a floured pastry board and divide into 5 parts. Roll out each into a 9-inch circle (use a cake pan as a guide). Place tortes on a greased baking sheet; bake 2 at a time in a preheated oven at 350° for 15 to 20 minutes or until light golden.

To prepare filling, mix potato starch in ½ cup milk. Put the remaining milk and sugar into a pan and bring to a boil. Beat in potato starch mixture with a wire whisk. Bring to a full boil; remove from heat. Cool completely. Cream butter with cocoa in a separate bowl; blend into first mixture. Spread filling between torte layers, and spread additional filling over sides. Decorate top and sides with chopped nuts. Refrigerate for 6 to 8 hours.

ICINGS, FILLINGS, AND FLAVORINGS

SUGAR STAGES AND TEMPERATURES
VAŘENÍ CUKRU

To prepare basic sirup, use equal amounts of sugar and water.

THREAD (230°F. to 234°F.): Sirup spins a 2-inch thread when dropped from a fork or spoon.

SOFT BALL (234°F. to 240°F.): Sirup, when dropped into very cold water, forms a soft ball, which flattens when removed from water.

FIRM BALL (244°F. to 248°F.): Sirup, when dropped into very cold water, forms a firm ball, which does not flatten when removed from water.

HARD BALL (250°F. to 266°F.): Sirup, when dropped into very cold water, forms a ball that is hard enough to hold its shape, yet is pliable.

SOFT CRACK (270°F. to 290°F.): Sirup, when dropped into very cold water, separates into threads that are hard but not brittle.

HARD CRACK (300°F. to 310°F.): Sirup, when dropped into very cold water, separates into threads that are hard and brittle.

CLEAR LIQUID (320°F.): The sugar liquefies.

CARAMEL (BROWN LIQUID) (338°F.): The liquid becomes brown.

WATER ICING
VODOVÁ POLEVA

2 cups confectioners'
   sugar
2–3 tablespoons boiling
   water

Sift sugar into a bowl; add water. Stir with a wooden spoon until white and thick.

LEMON WATER ICING
CITRÓNOVÁ POLEVA

Add 2 tablespoons strained lemon juice to Water Icing (above).

ORANGE WATER ICING
POMERANČOVÁ POLEVA

Add 3 tablespoons strained orange juice to Water Icing (above).

RASPBERRY WATER ICING
MALINOVÁ POLEVA

Add 3 tablespoons raspberry sirup to Water Icing (above).

RUM (PUNCH) WATER ICING
RUMOVÁ (PUNCŎVÁ) POLEVA

Add 3 tablespoons rum to Water Icing (above).

WHITE ICING
BÍLKOVÁ POLEVA (LED)

1⅔ cups confectioners'
    sugar
2 egg whites

1 teaspoon strained
    lemon juice

Stir all ingredients until smooth and thick. You may vary the flavors as in Water Icing (above).

YOLK ICING
ŽLOUTKOVÁ POLEVA

3 egg yolks
1 cup confectioners' sugar
1 teaspoon vanilla

Beat all ingredients to a thick foam. The icing will dry quicker and better if poured over warm pastry.

CHOCOLATE ICING
ČOKOLÁDOVÁ POLEVA

¾ cup sugar
3 tablespoons water

3½ ounces (squares)
    chocolate, melted
1 tablespoon butter

Cook sugar and water together until mixture spins a thread (see Sugar Stages and Temperatures). Cream butter with chocolate in a bowl; slowly pour in sirup, beating constantly. Continue to beat icing until thick enough to spread. Use immediately. This icing sets quickly.

COCOA ICING
KAKAOVÁ POLEVA

6 tablespoons butter
⅔ cup confectioners' sugar
2 tablespoons cocoa

1 tablespoon milk
2 tablespoons potato
   starch

Melt butter. Stir in sugar; mix until smooth. Heat over a low flame. Add cocoa and milk, and bring just to boiling point but do not let icing boil. Add potato starch, and blend well. Remove from heat and use.

FONDANT ICING
FONDANTOVÁ POLEVA

1½ cups sugar
1 cup water
1 teaspoon vinegar

Cook sugar and water to 238°F. (soft-ball stage). Sprinkle with vinegar, and let cool without stirring. When mixture has cooled, start mixing it, stirring in only one direction. The fondant will first be thin, then it will thicken, then it will thin out again. When it starts to thicken a second time, pour it onto a marble slab or a baking sheet. Work into a ball. Let fondant ripen at least 24 hours in an airtight jar, then transfer to a double boiler. Add any desired flavoring or color, and heat to lukewarm. If fondant is too thick to use, add hot water, a teaspoonful at a time. Pour immediately over pastry; it sets quickly.
Covers 1 medium-sized cake.

VANILLA SUGAR
TLUČENÍ VANILKY

Wrap a vanilla bean in foil and dry in the oven until brittle. Break into small pieces and beat in a mortar with 2 or 3 sugar cubes to a fine powder. Sift. Keep in an airtight jar. Mix with confectioners' sugar, and use for dusting over cakes and pies.

COFFEE FLAVORING
KÁVOVÝ EXTRAKT

Add 3 tablespoons very finely ground coffee to ¼ cup boiling water. Cover, remove from heat, and let stand for 10 minutes. Strain through a piece of muslin.

YOLK PASTRY CREAM
ŽLOUTKOVÝ KRÉM

2 cups milk	2–3 egg yolks
6 tablespoons cornstarch	¾–1 cup sugar
½ teaspoon ground vanilla bean	½ cup Whipped Cream (see Index) or 1 egg white, stiffly beaten

Mix together all ingredients except Whipped Cream. Place in a hot-water bath, and beat with a wire whisk until thick. Cool. Fold in Whipped Cream or egg white.

BASIC BUTTER CREAM ICING I
MÁSLOVY KRÉM

1 cup butter
1 cup superfine sugar
2 eggs

Cream butter and sugar together thoroughly. Add eggs, 1 at a time, beating after each addition until mixture is fluffy.

Makes enough to fill and frost a 9-inch cake. Use ½ recipe for filling only.

BASIC BUTTER CREAM ICING II
MÁSLOVÝ KRÉM

3 tablespoons cornstarch
   or ½ package pre-
   pared pudding mix
   or ½ cup instantized
   flour

1 cup milk
1 cup butter
1 cup superfine sugar
2 egg yolks

In a bowl, mix cornstarch (or pudding or flour) with ⅛ cup milk. Bring remaining milk to a boil; add cornstarch mixture, and bring to a full boil, stirring constantly. Remove from heat and cool. Cream butter thoroughly with sugar and egg yolk. Add cool (but not cold) pudding to it by spoonfuls.

Note: Butter Cream Icing will curdle if:

you add too much liquid at once,
you add pudding when it is too cold,
you add too much pudding at once,
cream gets cold and you stir it.

To correct curdled Butter Cream Icing:

Heat bowl containing butter cream mixture over boiling water, and beat again.

Or cream 2 tablespoons butter with 2 tablespoons sugar, and add curdled butter cream to it by spoonfuls, beating constantly, until icing is thick enough to spread.

VANILLA BUTTER CREAM ICING
VANILKOVÝ

Prepare Butter Cream Icing I or II (above). Add ¼ teaspoon ground vanilla bean.

FRUIT BUTTER CREAM ICING
OVOCNÝ

Prepare Butter Cream Icing (above), but use less sugar in the basic recipe. Add 2 tablespoons jam or well-drained chopped stewed fruit, and blend well.

COFFEE BUTTER CREAM ICING
KÁVOVÝ

Prepare Butter Cream Icing (above). Bring 1 tablespoon ground coffee and 2 tablespoons water to a boil. Cool and strain. Add by drops to cream, beating constantly.

COCOA BUTTER CREAM ICING
KAKAOVÝ

Prepare Butter Cream Icing (above). Add ¼ cup cocoa, mixed with 1 to 2 tablespoons warm water or milk. Beat in well.

CHOCOLATE BUTTER CREAM ICING
ČOKOLÁDOVÝ

Prepare Butter Cream Icing (above). Beat in 3½ ounces melted chocolate.

FILBERT BUTTER CREAM ICING
OŘÍŠKOVÝ

Add 4 tablespoons ground Toasted Filberts (see Index) to Butter Cream Icing (above).

COFFEE NUT BUTTER CREAM ICING
OŘÍŠKO KÁVOVÝ

Add ¼ cup ground Toasted Filberts (see Index) to Coffee Butter Cream Icing (above).

WALNUT BUTTER CREAM ICING
OŘECHOVÝ

Add 4 to 5 tablespoons ground walnuts to Vanilla Butter Cream Icing (above).

VANILLA CREAM FILLING
VANILKOVÝ KRÉM

2 egg yolks
½ cup plus 2 tablespoons
   superfine sugar

½ teaspoon ground vanilla
   bean
2 tablespoons milk
1 cup butter

Beat egg yolks with sugar until foamy. Add vanilla and milk. Bring almost to a boil, but do not boil, stirring constantly. Pour into a bowl and cool. Cream butter, and to it add egg mixture, a spoonful at a time.

COFFEE CREAM FILLING
KÁVOVÝ KRÉM

Prepare Vanilla Cream (above), but add ½ cup very strong black coffee with the milk.

CHOCOLATE CREAM FILLING
ČOKOLÁDOVÝ KRÉM

Prepare Vanilla Cream (above), but add 2 ounces grated chocolate (bitter or sweet) with the milk.

COCOA CREAM FILLING
KAKAOVÝ KRÉM

Prepare Vanilla Cream (above), but add 2 tablespoons cocoa with the milk.

PARISIAN CREAM
KRÉM PAŘÍŽSKÝ

1 pound chocolate, grated
2 cups heavy cream

Bring cream and chocolate to a boil. Remove from heat and cool quickly by placing pan in a bowl of ice water. Refrigerate for 6 to 8 hours. Whip to a cream.

WHIPPED CREAM
ŠLEHANÁ SMETANA

2 cups heavy cream
3–4 tablespoons
        confectioners' sugar

Chill bowl and beater. Pour in cream, and whip until it stands in rounded peaks. Sift sugar over top, and fold in.

CHOCOLATE WHIPPED CREAM
ČOKOLÁDOVÁ ŠLEHANÁ SMETANA

Fold 3½ ounces grated chocolate (bitter or sweet) into 1 recipe Whipped Cream (above).

VANILLA WHIPPED CREAM
VANILKOVÁ ŠLEHANÁ SMETANA

Fold ½ teaspoon ground vanilla bean into 1 recipe Whipped Cream (above).

COCOA WHIPPED CREAM
KAKAOVÁ ŠLEHANÁ SMETANA

Mix 2 tablespoons cocoa with 1 tablespoon butter and 1 tablespoon Whipped Cream. Fold into rest of cream.

STRAWBERRY WHIPPED CREAM
JAHODOVÁ ŠLEHANÁ SMETANA

Fold ½ cup crushed strawberries into 1 recipe Whipped Cream (above).

COFFEE WHIPPED CREAM
KÁVOVÁ ŠLEHANÁ SMETANA

Gently blend 1 tablespoon very strong black coffee into 1 recipe Whipped Cream (above).

WHIPPED CREAM WITH EGG WHITES
ŠLEHANÁ SMETANA NASTAVENÁ BÍLKY

1 cup heavy cream	2 egg whites
2 tablespoons confectioners' sugar	6 tablespoons superfine sugar

Whip cream in a chilled bowl, using chilled beater. Sift confectioners' sugar over top; fold in gently. Beat egg whites until stiff; add superfine sugar, beating constantly until very stiff and glossy. Fold gently into whipped cream.

MOCK WHIPPED CREAM
NEPRAVÁ ŠLEHAČKA Z BÍLKŮ

3 egg whites
3 to 5 tablespoons
confectioners' sugar

2 or 3 tablespoons butter,
melted and cooled

Beat egg whites until stiff. Fold in sugar and butter. Use immediately, as this filling does not keep well.

NUT FILLING
OŘECHOVÁ NÁDIVKA

2 cups ground walnuts
⅔ cup sugar
1 teaspoon vanilla

2 tablespoons cream
2 eggs, separated

Mix together thoroughly walnuts, sugar, vanilla, cream, and egg yolks. Fold in stiffly beaten egg whites.
Makes about 2 cups.

FILBERT FILLING
NÁDIVKA Z LÍSKOVÝCH OŘÍŠKŮ

1 cup Toasted Filberts
(see Index)
4 teaspoons (approximately) water

½ teaspoon vanilla
1 tablespoon rum
(optional)

Grind nuts, add all other ingredients, and blend well. For a different flavor, add rum.
Makes about 1 cup.

POPPY SEED FILLING
MAKOVÁ NÁDIVKA

2 cups ground poppy
    seeds
¾ cup milk
⅔ cup sugar
2 tablespoons butter
1 teaspoon vanilla
½ teaspoon cinnamon

½ teaspoon grated lemon
    peel
2 tablespoons grated
    chocolate (bitter or
    sweet) or honey or
    jam (optional)
1 egg, separated
    (optional)

Simmer poppy seeds in milk, stirring constantly, for 5 minutes. Stir in sugar, butter, vanilla, cinnamon, lemon peel; simmer 5 minutes longer. Blend in chocolate, honey, or jam. Or cool filling, blend in egg yolk, and fold in stiffly beaten egg white.

Makes about 1½ to 2 cups filling.

APPLE FILLING
JABLKOVÁ NÁDIVKA

4 cups apples, pared and
    diced
¾ cup sugar
¼ cup water
1 tablespoon lemon juice

½ teaspoon grated lemon
    peel
¼ teaspoon cinnamon
1 tablespoon rum
    fine bread crumbs
    (optional)

Cook apples until soft with all other ingredients except rum and bread crumbs. Rub through a sieve, or mash with a fork. Add rum. If filling is too thin, add some fine bread crumbs.

Makes about 2 cups.

PRUNE BUTTER FILLING
POVIDLOVÁ NÁDIVKA

1 cup prune butter
2 tablespoons warm
    water or rum
⅓–½ cup sugar

½ teaspoon cinnamon
½ teaspoon grated lemon
    peel or orange peel

Mix prune butter with water or rum. Add all other ingredients and blend.

CHEESE FILLING
TVAROHOVÁ NÁDIVKA

1 pound farmer cheese
¼ cup butter
½ cup sugar
2 eggs, separated

1–2 teaspoons vanilla
½ cup raisins
1–2 tablespoons milk or
    cream

Rub cheese through a sieve. Cream butter, sugar, and egg yolks. Add cheese, vanilla, and raisins, and blend well. If mixture is too thick, add milk or cream. Fold in stiffly beaten egg whites.

COCOA FILLING
KAKAOVÁ NÁDIVKA

½ cup cocoa
⅓ cup sugar

¼ cup milk
1 teaspoon vanilla

Mix cocoa with sugar. Add milk and vanilla, and heat to a smooth thick cream, stirring constantly. This type of filling is used in yeast roll or Strudel (see Index), baked on a baking sheet or in a fluted tube pan.

CRUMB TOPPING
DROBENKA

1 cup instantized flour
½ cup sugar
6 tablespoons butter

Mix flour and sugar. Rub in butter until mixture forms crumbs. Chill before using.

COOKED MERINGUE FILLING
BÍLKOVÝ SNÍH VAŘENY V PÁŘE

4 egg whites
1 cup superfine sugar

Beat egg whites until stiff. Beat in sugar, a little at a time. Place in a hot-water bath and continue to beat until thickened. Remove from water; beat until cool.

DESSERTS AND DESSERT SAUCES

FRUIT CREAM
OVOCNÝ KRÉM

1 cup milk
2 egg yolks
¼ cup sugar
1 tablespoon cornstarch
2 tablespoons cognac
2 cups Whipped Cream
  (see Index)

⅔ cup chopped toasted
  nuts
1 orange, sliced
½ cup candied cherries
½ cup grapes

Mix together milk, egg yolks, sugar, and cornstarch. Bring to a full boil, stirring constantly. Cool. Add cognac and half the Whipped Cream. Fold in nuts and fruit. Pour into a mold, and chill until firm. Decorate with the remaining Whipped Cream. Serves 6.

FRUIT MERINGUE CREAM
OVOCNÝ KRÉM SNĚHOVÝ

6 apples
1 cup water
2 tablespoons raspberry
  or strawberry jam

⅓ cup sugar
1 lemon, juice only
2 egg whites, stiffly beaten

Bake apples in water in a 300° oven for about 1 hour. Rub through a sieve; cool. Mix sauce with jam, sugar, and lemon juice. Add beaten egg whites. Beat until thick. Chill. Serves 4 to 6.

APPLE CREAM
JABLKOVÝ KRÉM

3–4 apples
1 cup water
½ cup sugar

2 cups Whipped Cream
(see Index)
20 ladyfingers

Bake apples in water with sugar in a preheated 300° oven for about 1 hour. Rub through a sieve and cool. Fold in Whipped Cream. Line bottom of a deep serving dish with half the ladyfingers. Cover with cream and decorate with the remaining ladyfingers. Chill. Serves 4 to 6.

CHESTNUT CREAM
KAŠTANOVÝ KRÉM

2 pounds chestnuts
2 cups milk
½ cup sugar

1 teaspoon vanilla
1 cup Whipped Cream
(see Index)

Peel chestnuts. Boil in milk until soft (about ⅓ hour). Rub through a sieve. Add sugar and vanilla; stir constantly until cool (to prevent skin from forming on top). Fold in Whipped Cream. Serve immediately.

LEMON CREAM
CITRÓNOVÝ KRÉM

3 eggs, separated
½ cup sugar
juice of 1 lemon

grated lemon peel
(from ½ lemon)

Beat egg yolks with sugar until foamy. Add lemon juice and peel. Fold in stiffly beaten egg whites. Chill. Serves 4 to 5.

NUT CREAM
OŘÍŠKOVÝ KRÉM

1 cup ground Toasted
   Filberts (see Index)
½ cup plus 1 tablespoon
   superfine sugar
¼ cup cocoa

2 cups heavy cream
1 teaspoon vanilla
¼ cup Toasted Filberts
   (see Index), chopped

Mix ground filberts with sugar and cocoa. Add cream and vanilla. Beat to a thick foam. Pour into sherbet glasses, sprinkle with chopped nuts, and serve immediately. Serves 6 to 8.

CHOCOLATE MERINGUE CREAM
ČOKOLÁDOVÝ SNĚHOVÝ KRÉM

4 squares chocolate, melted
2 tablespoons warm milk

3 egg yolks
4 egg whites, stiffly beaten

Mix chocolate with milk until smooth. Add egg yolks, one at a time, beating well after each addition. Fold in egg whites. Chill. Serves 4 to 5.

CARAMEL CREAM
KARAMELOVÝ KRÉM

½ cup sugar
½ cup boiling water
1 cup milk or cream
1 teaspoon cornstarch

2 egg yolks
1 teaspoon vanilla
½–1 cup Whipped Cream
   (see Index)

Brown sugar to caramel (see Sugar Stages and Temperatures). Add boiling water and heat until caramel dissolves, stirring constantly. Pour in milk mixed with cornstarch, egg yolks, and vanilla. Heat in a double boiler until thickened, beating constantly with a wire whisk. Do not boil. Pour into sherbet glasses; chill until firm. Top with Whipped Cream before serving. Serves 4.

COCOA MERINGUE CREAM
KAKAOVÝ SNĚHOVÝ KRÉM

2 tablespoons cocoa	2 eggs, separated
1 tablespoon lukewarm milk	¼ cup sugar
	1 tablespoon water

Mix cocoa with milk. Add egg yolks, and beat until creamy. Sprinkle sugar with water and cook to soft crack (see Sugar Stages and Temperatures). Beat egg whites until stiff. Slowly pour in sirup, beating constantly; continue to beat until cool. Fold into egg-yolk mixture. Mound in individual serving dishes and decorate with cookies. Chill. Serves 2.

ORANGE GELÉE
POMERANČOVÝ ROSOL

1 cup sugar	4 egg yolks
6 tablespoons white wine	2½ tablespoons gelatin
2 oranges, juice only	2 tablespoons rum
1 lemon, juice only	5 egg whites, stiffly beaten
1 tablespoon grated orange peel	

Sprinkle sugar with wine, add orange juice, lemon juice, orange peel, and egg yolks. Beat over low heat until thickened. Stir in gelatin softened in rum, and cool. Fold in egg whites. Pour into a rinsed mold, and chill until firm. Serves 6 to 8.

STRAWBERRY CREAM
JAHODOVÝ KRÉM

1 cup milk	2 tablespoons cognac
2 egg yolks	3 cups Whipped Cream
¼ cup sugar	(see Index)
1 tablespoon cornstarch	3 cups strawberries

Mix together milk, egg yolks, sugar, and cornstarch. Bring to a full boil, stirring constantly. Let mixture cool, then add cognac and 2 cups Whipped Cream. Place 1 cup strawberries in a mold, pour in half the cream; repeat process. Chill until firm. Decorate with the remaining strawberries and Whipped Cream. Serves 8.

VANILLA ICE CREAM I
VANILKOVÁ ZMRZLINA

4 cups milk	2½ tablespoons cornstarch
4 egg yolks	1 vanilla bean
1 cup sugar	

Mix together all ingredients until well blended. Heat in a double boiler, beating constantly with a wire whisk. Cook to a thick cream, but do not boil. Remove from heat; strain to remove vanilla bean. Beat until cool. Turn into a refrigerator tray and freeze, stirring every 30 minutes, until firm. Serves 8 to 10.

VANILLA ICE CREAM II
VANILKOVÁ ZMRZLINA

4 cups cream or milk	1 cup sugar
6–8 egg yolks	1 vanilla bean

Prepare like Vanilla Ice Cream I. Serves 8 to 10.

NUT ICE CREAM
OŘÍŠKOVÁ ZMRZLINA

Prepare Vanilla Ice Cream I or II, but add ⅓ cup Toasted Filberts (see Index), chopped or ground, to cooled mixture. Serves 8 to 10.

COFFEE ICE CREAM
KÁVOVÁ ZMRZLINA

Prepare Vanilla Ice Cream I or II, but use 3 cups milk and 1 cup very strong black coffee for the liquid. Serves 8 to 10.

CHOCOLATE ICE CREAM
ČOKOLÁDOVÁ ZMRZLINA

Prepare Vanilla Ice Cream II, but add 3½ ounces (squares) melted chocolate to cooled mixture. Serves 8 to 10.

RUM CHARLOTTE RUSSE
RUMOVÝ KRÉM

1 cup milk	2½ tablespoons gelatin
4 eggs, separated	½ cup rum
1 cup sugar	30 ladyfingers

Mix together milk, egg yolks, and sugar. Beat over low heat until thickened. Add gelatin softened in rum, and chill. Fold in stiffly beaten egg whites. Line bottom and sides of a form with ladyfingers. Pour in cream mixture, and chill until firm. Serves 6 to 8.

VANILLA PUDDING
VANILKOVÝ PUDINK

2 cups milk
⅓ cup sugar
2-inch piece vanilla bean

5 tablespoons potato
  starch
1 egg white, stiffly beaten

Heat 1½ cups of the milk with sugar and vanilla bean. Mix together remaining milk and potato starch, and pour into hot mixture, stirring constantly. Bring to full boil. Remove from heat. Take out vanilla bean. Mix in egg white. Pour into individual molds and chill. Unmold on individual dishes and serve with fruit sirup or any dessert sauce or cream (see Index). Serves 4.

COFFEE PUDDING (MOCHA PUDDING)
KÁVOVÝ PUDINK

Prepare like Cocoa Pudding (below), but substitute 1 cup strong black coffee for half the milk. Serves 4.

NUT PUDDING
OŘÍŠKOVÝ PUDINK

2 cups milk
½ cup sugar
1 teaspoon vanilla
5 tablespoons cornstarch

1 egg, separated
⅔ cup ground toasted nuts
  whole or halved nuts
  for decoration

Pour 1½ cups of the milk, sugar, and vanilla into a saucepan and bring to a boil. Mix remaining milk thoroughly with cornstarch and egg yolk. Pour into hot mixture, stirring constantly. Bring to a boil again. Cool. Fold in ground nuts and stiffly beaten egg white. Pour into serving dishes; decorate with nuts, and chill. Serves 4 to 6.

COCOA PUDDING
KAKAOVÝ PUDINK

Prepare like Vanilla Pudding (above), but add 1 to 2 tablespoons cocoa to the milk and sugar mixture. Serves 4.

FRUIT SHERBET
OVOCNÁ ZMRZLINA

2 cups water
1¼ cups sugar
1 tablespoon gelatin
2 cups fruit juice or
    puréed fruit

1 cup Whipped Cream
    (see Index;
    optional)

Soften gelatin in 2 tablespoons water. Pour balance of water over sugar; cook for 5 minutes. Stir in softened gelatin; cool. Add fruit juice (or puréed fruit) and Whipped Cream. Freeze until firm. Serves 8 to 10.

LEMON SHERBET
CITRÓNOVÁ ZMRZLINA

1½ cups water
1½ cups sugar

3 lemons, juice only
    grated peel from 1
    lemon

Pour water over sugar; cook for 5 minutes. Cool. Add lemon juice and peel. Freeze until firm. Serves 4.

TUTTI-FRUTTI SHERBET
ZMRZLINA TUTTI-FRUTTI

Prepare like Lemon Sherbet (above), but add 1 cup diced stewed fruit to mixture before freezing. Serves 4.

PUDDING MUSHROOMS
HŘIBY

2 cups milk
⅓ cup sugar
½ cup cornstarch
1 egg, separated
4 peaches or apricots

½ recipe Chocolate Icing
  (see Index)
Apricot Dessert Sauce
  (see Index)

Bring 1½ cups milk and sugar to a boil. Mix the remaining milk with cornstarch and egg yolk. Pour into hot mixture, stirring constantly. Bring to a boil. Cool. Fold in the stiffly beaten egg white. Pour into slim glasses rinsed with cold water and drained, and chill. Pour chocolate icing over peach or apricot halves. Let set. Unmold pudding into fruit dishes; place a peach (or apricot) half on top of each. Pour dessert sauce over each serving. Serves 8.

FARINA FLAMERI
KRUPICOVÉ FLAMERI

2 cups milk
½ cup sugar
1 teaspoon vanilla
  dash of salt

½ cup plus 1 tablespoon
  farina
2 egg whites, stiffly
  beaten
1–2 cups fruit

Bring milk, sugar, vanilla, and salt to a boil. Pour in farina, stirring constantly; cook for 10 minutes. Remove from heat and fold in egg whites. Chill in a ring mold rinsed with cold water and drained. Unmold, and fill center with either fresh or stewed fruit. Serve with fruit sirup, or fruit dessert sauce or with Caramel Cream (see Index). Serves 6.

CHOCOLATE OR COCOA FLAMERI
ČOKOLÁDOVÉ NEBO KAKAOVÉ FLAMERI

Prepare like Farina Flameri (above), but add 2 ounces (squares) grated chocolate or 3 tablespoons cocoa to the milk. Serves 6.

ALMOND MOUSSE
ZMRZLÝ MANDLOVÝ KRÉM

1⅓ cups ground Blanched Almonds (see Index)	½ cup sugar
	1½ cups Whipped Cream (see Index)
½ cup milk	1 tablespoon cocoa
2 tablespoons gelatin	
¼ cup water	

Cook almonds and milk for about 10 minutes. Soften gelatin in water, and add to hot mixture. Cool. Add sugar and Whipped Cream. Pour half the mixture into a mold rinsed with cold water and chill until firm. Mix cocoa into the other half of the mixture, and pour over first mixture after it is firm. Freeze for 2 to 3 hours. Dip bottom of mold into hot water, turn mousse out on a platter. Serves 6.

STRAWBERRY MOUSSE
ZMRZLÝ JAHODOVÝ KRÉM

2 tablespoons gelatin	2 cups Whipped Cream (see Index)
6 tablespoons boiling water	whole strawberries (for decoration; optional)
2 cups strawberries	
¾ cup sugar	

Dissolve gelatin in water. Rub strawberries through a sieve; stir in sugar. Add liquid gelatin and cream. Pour into a mold rinsed with cold water, and freeze for 2 to 3 hours. Dip bottom of mold into hot water, and turn out on a platter. Decorate with additional strawberries, if desired. Serves 4 to 6.

APRICOT MOUSSE
ZMRZLÝ MERUŇKOVÝ KRÉM

6 tablespoons sugar
½ cup white wine
10 large apricots, peeled
　　and pitted
1 egg white
½ cup ground Blanched
　　Almonds (see Index)

2 tablespoons gelatin
2 cups Whipped Cream
　　(see Index)
apricot halves (for
　　decoration; optional)

Sprinkle sugar with 6 tablespoons of white wine and bring to a boil. Add apricots. Cook for about 10 minutes, or until soft. Rub through a sieve; cool. Add egg white, and beat to a thick foam. Blend in almonds. Dissolve gelatin by heating it in the remaining wine, and add to fruit mixture. Blend in cream. Pour into a mold rinsed with cold water and freeze for 2 to 3 hours. Dip bottom of mold into hot water, and turn out on a platter. Decorate with additional apricot halves, if desired. Serves 4 to 6.

TUTTI-FRUTTI MOUSSE
ZMRZLÝ OVOCNÝ KRÉM

1 cup milk
3 egg yolks
½ cup sugar
1 teaspoon vanilla
3 tablespoons gelatin

½ cup hot water
1 cup diced stewed fruit
1½ cups Whipped Cream
　　(see Index)
fruit for decoration
　　(optional)

Mix together egg yolks, sugar, and vanilla. Heat in a double boiler until thickened, beating constantly. Do not let boil. Add gelatin dissolved in water. Cool. Mix in fruit and 1 cup Whipped Cream. Pour into a mold rinsed with cold water and drained, and freeze for 2 to 3 hours. Dip bottom of mold into hot water; turn mousse out onto a platter. Decorate with remaining ½ cup Whipped Cream and fruit. Serves 4 to 6.

VANILLA MOUSSE
ZMRZLÝ VANILKOVÝ KRÉM

⅔ cup milk
3 egg yolks
¾ cup sugar
1 teaspoon potato starch
2½ tablespoons gelatin
¼ cup milk

3 tablespoons rum
2 teaspoons vanilla
1 cup Whipped Cream
   (see Index)
20 ladyfingers
⅓ cup apricot jam

Mix together ⅔ cup milk, egg yolks, sugar, and potato starch. Heat in a double boiler, beating constantly, until mixture has the consistency of thick cream. Add gelatin softened in ¼ cup milk; stir until dissolved. Cool. Fold in rum, vanilla, and Whipped Cream. Pour one third of mixture into a mold rinsed with cold water and drained. Spread half the ladyfingers with jam; top with the rest. Arrange half the ladyfinger sandwiches on the cream in the mold; pour half of the remaining cream over them; chill until firm. Arrange the remaining ladyfinger sandwiches on top, and pour on the remaining cream. Freeze for 2 to 3 hours. Dip mold in hot water, and turn out onto a platter. Serves 5.

STEAMED PUDDINGS
VAŘENÍ PUDINKU

A steamed pudding can be cooked either in a special form with a well-fitting cover or in an open form covered with foil. Both form and cover must be well greased with butter and sprinkled with fine bread crumbs or instantized flour, and the form must be filled only two thirds full. To steam pudding, place form in a vessel taller than itself and containing boiling water reaching one third up the form. Cover, and simmer over low heat for 45 to 60 minutes. Add more boiling water if necessary to maintain the water level.

STEAMED RICE PUDDING
RÝŽOVÝ PUDINK

⅓ cup rice
¼ cup ground almonds
2 cups milk
dash of salt

¼ cup butter
⅓ cup sugar
3 eggs, separated

Cook rice, almonds, and milk until rice is done (about 14 minutes). Mix in butter, and cool. Add sugar and egg yolks, 1 at a time, beating well after each addition. Fold in stiffly beaten egg whites. Steam for 45 minutes (see Steamed Puddings, above, for method). Serve with stewed apricots and sirup. Serves 4 to 6.

STEAMED CHERRY PUDDING
ŽEMLOVÝ PUDINK TŘEŠŇOVÝ

3 stale hard rolls, diced
½ cup milk
⅓ cup ground nuts or
    Blanched Almonds
    (see Index)
6 tablespoons butter
    dash of salt
1 teaspoon grated lemon
    peel

½ cup sugar
¼ teaspoon cinnamon
4 eggs, separated
1 pound cherries, pitted
    Cherry or Wine
    Dessert Sauce
    (see Index)

Sprinkle milk over rolls and let stand for 20 minutes. Mix in almonds, butter, salt, lemon peel, sugar, and cinnamon. Simmer for about 2 minutes. Cool, stirring occasionally. Beat in egg yolks well, one at a time, and half the cherries. Fold in stiffly beaten egg whites. Steam for 1 hour (see Steamed Puddings for method). Serve with the remaining cherries and Cherry or Wine Dessert Sauce. Serves 6.

STEAMED MERINGUE PUDDING
SNĚHOVÝ PUDINK

4 egg whites, stiffly beaten	¼ cup instantized flour
6 tablespoons sugar	1 teaspoon grated lemon
½ cup ground nuts	peel

Fold dry ingredients into egg whites. Steam for 35 to 40 minutes (see Steamed Puddings for method). Serve with raspberry sirup. Serves 4.

STEAMED QUEEN'S PUDDING
KRÁLOVNIN PUDINK

JELLY ROLL	PUDDING
2 eggs, separated	5 tablespoons butter
¼ cup sugar	5 tablespoons sugar
½ cup flour	4 eggs, separated
½ cup jam	1 tablespoon cocoa
¼ cup milk	dash of cinnamon
	dash of ground cloves
	½ cup ground filberts
	⅔ cup Dry Cake Crumbs
	(see Index)

To prepare Jelly Roll, beat egg whites until stiff. Add sugar, a little at a time. Mix in egg yolks and flour. Pour into a small greased baking pan lined with waxed paper. Bake in a preheated 350° oven for about 15 minutes. Turn out onto a damp towel; peel off paper. Spread with jam; roll up. Chill. Slice, line a greased pudding form with slices, and sprinkle them with milk.

To prepare pudding, cream butter with sugar until light. Add egg yolks, 1 at a time, beating well after each addition, then mix in cocoa, cinnamon, cloves, and filberts. Fold in stiffly beaten egg whites alternately with cake crumbs. Pour over Jelly Roll into pudding form, and steam for 1 hour (see Steamed Puddings for method). Serve with any fruit dessert sauce (see Index). Serves 8 to 10.

STEAMED COFFEE PUDDING
KÁVOVÝ PUDINK

1½ cups boiling milk
½ cup finely ground
    coffee
½ cup butter

1 cup instantized flour
½ cup sugar
4 eggs, separated
    Coffee Cream (see
    Index)

Pour milk over coffee. Cover, and let cool. Melt butter, add flour to it, and blend well. Pour in strained coffee-milk, blend, and cook until smooth. Add sugar and egg yolks, one at a time, beating well after each addition. Fold in stiffly beaten egg whites. Steam for 1 hour (see Steamed Puddings for method). Serve with Coffee Cream. Serves 6.

STEAMED CHEESE PUDDING
TVAROHOVÝ PUDINK

⅓ cup butter
⅓ cup sugar
4 eggs, separated
½ cup plus 1 tablespoon
    farmer cheese, sieved

⅓ cup raisins
½ teaspoon grated lemon
    peel
½ cup farina

Cream butter and sugar. Add egg yolks, 1 at a time, beating each in well. Add cheese, raisins, and lemon peel. Fold in stiffly beaten egg whites and farina. Steam for 1 hour (see Steamed Puddings for method). Serve with melted butter or stewed fruit. Serves 6.

STEAMED CHESTNUT PUDDING
KAŠTANOVÝ PUDINK

½ pound chestnuts,
  peeled
1⅓ cups milk
1 teaspoon vanilla

⅓ cup sugar
5 tablespoons butter
4 eggs, separated
  Vanilla Cream (see
  Index)

Cook chestnuts in milk until soft (about ½ hour). Rub through a sieve. Add vanilla, sugar, and butter. Simmer for 5 minutes. Cool. Add egg yolks, 1 at a time, beating well after each addition; then fold in stiffly beaten egg whites. Steam for 1 hour (see Steamed Puddings for method). Serve with Vanilla Cream. Serves 6 to 8.

STEAMED CHOCOLATE PUDDING
ČOKOLÁDOVÝ PUDINK

¾ cup sugar
4 eggs, separated
3½ ounces (squares)
  chocolate, grated
6 tablespoons instantized
  flour

1 cup ground nuts
  Whipped Cream with
  Egg Whites (see
  Index)

Beat sugar and egg yolks until foamy. Add chocolate. Fold in stiffly beaten egg whites and flour mixed with nuts. Steam for 45 minutes (see Steamed Puddings for method). Serve with Whipped Cream with Egg Whites. Serves 6.

STEAMED CARAMEL PUDDING
KARAMELOVÝ PUDINK

½ cup sugar
3 tablespoons water
1½ cups milk
½ cup butter

1 cup instantized flour
4 eggs, separated
Caramel Cream (see Index)

Sprinkle sugar with water and cook to caramel (see Sugar Stages and Temperatures). Remove from heat, pour in milk, and cook until caramel dissolves. Cool. Melt butter, blend flour into it. Pour in caramel mixture and cook until smooth. Cool. Add egg yolks, one at a time, beating each in well. Fold in stiffly beaten egg whites. Steam for 1 hour (see Steamed Puddings for method). Serve with Caramel Cream. Serves 6.

FRIED FRUIT
SMAŽENÉ OVOCE

fruit
2 tablespoons rum
2 egg yolks
1 cup milk

dash of salt
1 tablespoon sugar
1 cup instantized flour
shortening for frying

Sprinkle fruit (see type and quantity below), and let stand for a few minutes. Beat together egg yolks, milk, salt, sugar, and flour. Dip fruit into batter, then fry in hot shortening to a golden brown.

Use 4 peaches or 8 to 12 apricots. Cut in half before frying.

Use 3 to 4 apples or pears. Peel, core, and cut in ½-inch-thick slices before frying.

Use 2 to 3 cups blueberries, strawberries, red currants, pitted cherries (sweet or sour), or fresh prunes. Add rum to batter instead of to fruit; mix in fruit, and drop by spoonfuls into hot fat.

PEACH PORCUPINES
BROSKVOVÍ JEŽCI

Sponge Cake (see
   Index) 9 by 9 inches
   square
8 peaches, halved

½ cup slivered Blanched
   Almonds (see Index)
Chocolate Icing (see
   Index)

Lay peaches on sponge cake, cut side down. Stick in almond slivers, porcupine style. Cover with chocolate icing, and chill. Cut into squares to serve.

STEWED FRUIT
RYCHLÝ KOMPOT

⅓–¾ cup sugar
   (depending on
   tartness of fruit)
1 cup water

½ lemon, juice only
   fruit (see below)

Pour water over sugar and bring to full boil. Add lemon juice and fruit. Cook as directed below. Remove fruit from liquid, continue to cook liquid until sirupy, then pour over fruit. Chill.

Blueberries, cranberries, gooseberries, strawberries, raspberries, blackberries, red currants, sweet or sour cherries, or fresh prunes: Use 2 to 3 cups. Cook for 2 minutes.

Peaches and apricots: Use 3 peaches (peel first by dipping in boiling water), cut in half and pitted, or 8 to 12 apricots. Cook for 2 to 3 minutes.

Apples and pears: Use 3 to 4, peeled, cored, and quartered. Add a strip of lemon peel or piece of cinnamon stick, or 1 whole clove during cooking. Cook for 3 minutes.

FILLED BAKED APPLES
PLNĚNÁ JABLKA

4 baking apples, peeled
and cored
2 tablespoons chopped
Blanched Almonds
(see Index) or other
nuts
⅓ cup raisins

2 tablespoons rum or
water
2 tablespoons cranberries
1 teaspoon grated lemon
peel
½ cup sugar
¼ cup water
1 tablespoon lemon juice

Sprinkle rum or 2 tablespoons water over raisins. Mix together almonds, raisins, cranberries, lemon peel, and half the sugar; fill cavity of each apple with mixture. Boil ¼ cup water with remaining sugar and lemon juice. Place apples in a baking dish, pour in sirup, and bake in a preheated 350° oven for 30 to 45 minutes. Serves 4.

BAKED APPLE FLUFF
JABLKOVÝ NÁKYP PĚNOVÝ

6 apples, pared, cored,
and sliced
½ cup white wine
1¼ cups sugar
1 teaspoon lemon juice

1 teaspoon grated lemon
peel
4 egg whites
confectioners' sugar

Cook apples in wine until soft; cool. Rub through a sieve. Add half the sugar, lemon juice and peel, and 1 egg white; beat to a thick foam. Beat the remaining egg whites until stiff, and beat in rest of sugar. Mix with apple foam, and beat together until very thick. Pile into a buttered pie pan, and bake in a preheated 350° oven for 15 to 25 minutes. Sprinkle with confectioners' sugar. Serve warm or chilled. Serves 4 to 6.

BAKED LEMON FLUFF
CITRÓNOVÝ NÁKYP PĚNOVÝ

3 eggs, separated
6 tablespoons superfine
  sugar

grated peel of 1 lemon
juice of ½ lemon
confectioners' sugar

Beat egg yolks with superfine sugar until foamy. Add lemon peel and juice. Fold in stiffly beaten egg whites. Pile into a buttered pie pan, and bake in a 325° oven for 15 to 25 minutes. Sprinkle with confectioners' sugar. Serve warm or chilled. Serves 4 to 6.

BAKED RASPBERRY FLUFF
MALINOVÝ NÁKYP PĚNOVÝ

1 cup raspberries, mashed
¾ cup superfine sugar
3 egg whites

½ teaspoon lemon juice
confectioners' sugar

Beat raspberries, ½ cup superfine sugar, 1 egg white, and lemon juice into a thick foam. Beat the remaining egg whites until stiff, then beat in ¼ cup superfine sugar. Fold into fruit foam. Pile into a buttered pie pan, and bake in a preheated 350° oven for 15 to 25 minutes. Sprinkle with confectioners' sugar. Serves 4 to 6.

BAKED STRAWBERRY FLUFF
JAHODOVÝ NÁKYP PĚNOVÝ

Make like Baked Raspberry Fluff (above), but use mashed strawberries in place of raspberries. Serves 4 to 6.

BAKED APRICOT FLUFF
MERUŇKOVÝ NÁKYP PĚNOVÝ

Make like Baked Raspberry Fluff (above), but use 6 mashed stewed apricots in place of raspberries. Serves 4 to 6.

DESSERT OMELET
OMELETA PIŠKOTOVÁ

4 eggs, separated	⅔ cup flour
⅓ cup sugar	¼ cup jam

Beat egg whites until stiff. Blend in egg yolks, 1 at a time, and sprinkle each with sugar and flour before adding it. Pour into 2 greased and floured pie plates. Bake in a preheated 300° oven for 7 to 10 minutes. Spread jam on top, and fold in half. Serves 2 to 4.

COCOA SOUFFLÉ
KAKAOVÝ NÁKYP

2½ tablespoons butter	3 eggs, separated
2 tablespoons instantized flour	¼ cup superfine sugar
1½ cups milk	1 tablespoon cocoa
	fine bread crumbs

Melt butter, blend in flour. Pour in milk, a little at a time, stirring constantly, until mixture becomes thick and smooth and does not stick to pan. Remove to a bowl, and cool. Mix in egg yolks, one at a time, beating well after each addition, and sugar mixed with cocoa. Fold in stiffly beaten egg whites. Pour into a greased soufflé dish sprinkled with bread crumbs. Bake in a preheated 325° oven for 45 minutes. Serves 4.

CHOCOLATE SOUFFLÉ
ČOKOLÁDOVÝ NÁKYP

3 eggs, separated
¼ cup superfine sugar
⅛ cup ground Blanched
  Almonds (see
  Index)
1¾ ounces (squares)
  chocolate, grated

1 tablespoon instantized
  flour
½ teaspoon grated lemon
  peel
dash of cinnamon
fine bread crumbs

Beat egg whites until stiff. Fold in lightly beaten egg yolks. Mix the remaining ingredients, and fold into eggs. Pour into a greased baking dish sprinkled with bread crumbs, and bake in a preheated 300° oven for 30 to 40 minutes. Serve with Wine Sauce (see Index). Serves 4.

NUT SOUFFLÉ
OŘECHOVÝ NÁKYP

3 eggs, separated
6 tablespoons superfine
  sugar
½ cup ground nuts
2 tablespoons instantized
  flour

2 tablespoons Dry Cake
  Crumbs (see Index)
½ teaspoon grated lemon
  peel
2 tablespoons rum
fine bread crumbs

Beat egg whites until stiff. Beat in sugar a little at a time, until whites are very stiff and glossy. Fold in lightly beaten egg yolks. Mix together nuts, flour, crumbs, and lemon peel; fold into eggs. Sprinkle with rum, and blend lightly. Pour into a greased baking dish sprinkled with bread crumbs and bake in a preheated 325° oven for about 45 minutes. Serve with Rum Sauce or Chocolate Sauce (see Index). Serves 4.

APPLE SOUFFLÉ
JABLKOVÝ NÁKYP

9 small apples, peeled,
 cored, and sliced
2 tablespoons white wine
7 tablespoons sugar
3 eggs, separated
¼ cup chopped citron

⅓ cup ground almonds or
 other nuts
2 tablespoons fine bread
 crumbs
 confectioners' sugar

Cook apples with wine and 2 tablespoons sugar until soft (about 5 minutes). Cool. Beat egg yolks with the remaining sugar until foamy. Add apples, citron, and nuts. Fold in stiffly beaten egg whites and the 2 tablespoons bread crumbs. Pour into a greased soufflé dish sprinkled with fine bread crumbs. Bake in a preheated 325° oven for 45 minutes. Sprinkle with confectioners' sugar. Serves 4 to 6.

FARINA SOUFFLÉ WITH WINE
KRUPICOVÝ NÁKYP S VÍNEM

SOUFFLE

3 eggs, separated
½ cup superfine sugar
⅔ cup farina
 fine bread crumbs

SAUCE

½ cup red wine
½ cup water
6 tablespoons sugar
 dash of cinnamon

To make the soufflé, beat egg whites until stiff. Beat in sugar, a little at a time, until whites are very stiff and glossy. Fold in lightly beaten egg yolks alternately with farina. Pour into a greased baking dish sprinkled with bread crumbs. Bake in a preheated 300° oven for 30 to 40 minutes.

While soufflé is baking, prepare sauce. Mix together wine, water, sugar, and cinnamon, and cook for 5 minutes. Pour over soufflé after removing it from oven, then return to oven to bake 10 minutes longer. Serves 3 to 4.

CAKE SOUFFLÉ
PIŠKOTOVÝ NÁKYP

3 eggs, separated
¾ cup superfine sugar

1⅓ cups instantized flour
fine bread crumbs

Beat egg whites until stiff. Beat in sugar by spoonfuls. Fold in lightly beaten egg yolks, then fold in flour. Pour into a greased baking dish sprinkled with fine bread crumbs. Bake in a preheated 300° oven for 30 to 40 minutes. Serve with Fruit Sauce, Vanilla Sauce, or Wine Sauce (see Index). Serves 3 to 4.

COFFEE DESSERT SAUCE
KÁVOVÝ KRÉM

½ cup milk or cream
¼ cup sugar
½ cup strong black coffee

2 egg yolks
1 teaspoon potato starch

Bring milk or cream and sugar to a boil. Remove from heat. Mix coffee, egg yolks, and potato starch thoroughly. Pour into boiled mixture. Heat in a double boiler, beating constantly, until thickened. Do not boil. Serves 3 to 4.

CHESTNUT DESSERT SAUCE
KAŠTANOVÝ KRÉM

½ pound chestnuts,
    peeled
1½ cups milk
1 teaspoon vanilla

3 tablespoons sugar
3 egg whites, stiffly
    beaten

Boil chestnuts in 1 cup milk for about 30 minutes or until soft. Rub through a sieve to purée. Add remaining milk and vanilla, and heat until thickened. Mix in sugar; fold in egg whites.

RUM OR MARASCHINO DESSERT SAUCE
RUMOVÝ NEBO MARASCHINOVÝ KRÉM

1 cup milk or cream	1 teaspoon potato starch
¼ cup sugar	¼ cup rum or juice from
3 egg yolks	maraschino cherries

Bring ¾ cup milk (or cream) and sugar to a boil. Remove from heat. Mix remaining milk with egg yolks and potato starch; pour into the boiled mixture. Heat in a double boiler, beating constantly, until thickened. Do not boil. Blend in rum or maraschino flavor.

VANILLA DESSERT SAUCE
VANILKOVÝ KRÉM

RECIPE I

1 cup milk or cream
¼ cup sugar
2 teaspoons vanilla
4 egg yolks

RECIPE II

1 cup milk
¼ cup sugar
2 teaspoons vanilla
2 egg yolks
1 teaspoon potato starch

For either recipe, mix ¾ cup milk (or cream) with sugar and vanilla. Bring to a boil. Remove from heat. Blend together remaining milk, well-beaten egg yolks (and potato starch, for Recipe II), and pour into the boiled mixture. Heat in a double boiler, beating constantly, until thickened. Do not boil.

COCOA DESSERT SAUCE
KAKAOVÝ KRÉM

1 cup milk	2 egg yolks
1 tablespoon cocoa	1 teaspoon potato starch
¼ cup sugar	

Mix together all ingredients. Heat in a double boiler, beating constantly, until thickened. Do not boil.

JAM DESSERT SAUCE
ZAVAŘENINOVÁ OMÁČKA

½ pound jam
1 cup water or ½ cup
    water plus ½ cup
    white wine

2 tablespoons sugar
1 teaspoon potato starch
2 tablespoons water

Mix jam, 1 cup water (or water-and-wine), and sugar together until smooth. Simmer for 5 minutes. Add potato starch mixed in 2 tablespoons water, and bring to a full boil, stirring constantly, until thickened. Serve warm over puddings or soufflés.

BLUEBERRY DESSERT SAUCE
BORŮVKOVÁ OMÁČKA (ŽAHOUR)

2 cups blueberries
1 cup water or milk
¼ cup sugar

1 tablespoon butter
1 teaspoon potato starch

Simmer blueberries in half the water or milk with sugar and butter for 10 to 15 minutes. Mix starch with the rest of the liquid, and add to blueberries. Bring to a full boil, stirring constantly. Serve warm over pancakes, unfilled yeast dumplings (see Index), or biscuits.

LEMON DESSERT SAUCE
CITRÓNOVÁ OMÁČKA

3 tablespoons butter
1 tablespoon flour
½ cup water
½ cup white wine
¼ cup sugar

grated peel of ½
    lemon
2–3 tablespoons lemon
    juice (1 lemon)
1 egg yolk, lightly
    beaten

Melt butter; blend in flour. Add water, wine, sugar, and half the lemon peel. Simmer for 5 minutes. Strain. Blend in the remaining lemon peel, lemon juice, and egg yolk. Serve warm over puddings or soufflés.

ORANGE DESSERT SAUCE I
POMERANČOVÁ OMÁČKA

Prepare like Lemon Dessert Sauce (above), but substitute orange peel and orange juice for lemon peel and lemon juice.

ORANGE DESSERT SAUCE II
POMERANČOVÁ PĚNA

1 cup white wine	⅔ cup (approximately)
4 egg yolks	orange juice
	⅓ cup sugar

Mix together all ingredients. Heat in a double boiler, beating constantly, until thickened and foamy. Do not boil. Serve immediately.

APRICOT DESSERT SAUCE
MERUŇKOVÁ OMÁČKA

4–6 apricots, halved and pitted	pinch of cinnamon or grated lemon peel
1 cup water	1 teaspoon potato starch
¾ cup sugar	2 tablespoons water

Simmer apricots, 1 cup water, sugar, and cinnamon or lemon peel for 20 to 30 minutes. Rub through a sieve. Add potato starch mixed in 2 tablespoons water and bring to a full boil, stirring constantly. Serve warm over puddings or soufflés.

CHERRY DESSERT SAUCE
TŘEŠŇOVÁ OMÁČKA

Prepare like Apricot Dessert Sauce (above), but substitute 1 cup of pitted cherries or sour cherries for apricots. Serve warm over puddings or soufflés.

RASPBERRY DESSERT SAUCE
MALINOVÁ OMÁČKA

2 cups raspberries, mashed	1 cup water
¾ cup sugar	1 teaspoon potato starch
	2 tablespoons water

Simmer raspberries, sugar, and 1 cup water for about 10 minutes. Add potato starch dissolved in 2 tablespoons water, and bring to a full boil, stirring constantly. Serve warm over puddings or soufflés.

STRAWBERRY DESSERT SAUCE
JAHODOVÁ OMÁČKA

2 cups strawberries, mashed	½ cup sugar
1 cup water	1 teaspoon vanilla

Mix together all ingredients and simmer for 10 to 15 minutes. Serve warm over puddings or soufflés.

WINE DESSERT SAUCE
VINNÁ PĚNA (ŠODÓ)

RECIPE I	RECIPE II
1 cup white wine	1 cup white wine
4 egg yolks	2 egg yolks
⅓ cup sugar	1 teaspoon potato starch
1 teaspoon vanilla	⅓ cup sugar
	1 teaspoon vanilla

For either recipe, whip together all ingredients. Heat in a double boiler, beating constantly, until thickened and foamy. Do not boil. Serve immediately.

SANDWICHES
AND SANDWICH SPREADS

PIQUANT HOT SANDWICHES
OPEČENÉ CHLEBÍČKY PIKANTNÍ

12 slices French bread, ½
    inch thick
6 tablespoons butter
2 tablespoons ketchup or
    mustard

6 slices ham
6 slices Swiss cheese

Spread bread first with butter, then with ketchup or mustard. Place a half slice of ham and a half slice of cheese on each. Bake on a cookie sheet in a preheated 400° oven until cheese is melted.

FRESH YEAST SPREAD
POMAZÁNKA Z DROŽDÍ

1 small onion, chopped
¼ cup butter
4 tablespoons (2 ounces)
    compressed yeast
    (see Explanatory
    Notes)
½ cup milk or soup

2 tablespoons fine bread
    crumbs
salt to taste
1 egg, lightly beaten
1 teaspoon minced
    parsley
¼ teaspoon mustard
1 pickle, chopped

Fry onion in butter. Add crumbled yeast. Brown lightly, stirring constantly. Add milk, bread crumbs, and salt. Mix until smooth. Remove from heat, mix in remaining ingredients. Serve on rye bread.

FISH SPREAD
POMAZÁNKA Z RYBY

2 herrings or 2 kippers or
1 can sardines
2 large pickles
2 hard-cooked eggs

½ cup butter
1–2 tablespoons lemon
juice

Grind together fish, pickles, and eggs. Cream butter; add the ground mixture and lemon juice; mix well. Serve on slices of Italian-style bread or small rolls.

SMOKED HERRING SPREAD
POMAZÁNKA Z UZENÁČŮ

½ cup butter
1 smoked herring, boned,
ground
1 small onion, chopped

1 tablespoon chopped
capers
⅓ cup chopped sauerkraut
½ teaspoon French
mustard

Cream butter; add the rest of the ingredients. Mix well.

SARDINE SPREAD
POMAZÁNKA ZE SARDINEK

½ cup butter
½ cup grated Swiss cheese
1 can sardines in oil,
mashed

¼ teaspoon paprika
salt to taste
1 small onion, chopped
lemon juice to taste

Cream butter, add cheese and sardines with oil. Add rest of the ingredients and mix well.

SANDWICH SPREAD FROM LEFTOVER MEAT
POMAZÁNKA ZE ZBYTKŮ MASA

1 small onion, chopped
¼ cup butter or chopped
    bacon
1 cup ground leftover
    roast or boiled meat
1 teaspoon mustard

salt to taste
pepper to taste
1 teaspoon Worcestershire
    sauce
⅓ cup chopped pickles

Fry onion in butter, add meat, and brown lightly. Cool.
Add all other ingredients; mix well. Fills 8 sandwiches.

SMOKED MEAT SANDWICH SPREAD
POMAZÁNKA Z UZENÉHO MASA

¼ cup butter, creamed
1 teaspoon mustard
1 teaspoon grated onion
½ teaspoon capers,
    chopped

1 hard-cooked egg, diced
1 cup cooked, diced
    smoked meat

Blend together all the ingredients. Fills 8 sandwiches.

BOLOGNA SANDWICH SPREAD
POMAZÁNKA ZE SALÁMU

6 tablespoons butter,
    creamed
½ pound Bologna (or any
    soft sausage) ground

1 teaspoon grated onion
1 anchovy, mashed
1 pickle, chopped

Blend together all the ingredients. Fills 8 sandwiches.

EGG SANDWICH SPREAD I
POMAZÁNKY Z VAJEC

3 hard-cooked eggs,
    chopped
¼ pound ham, chopped
5 tablespoons mayon-
    naise, or ¼ cup soft
    butter

salt to taste
lemon juice to taste
pickles

Blend together all ingredients. Decorate with sliced pickles.

EGG SANDWICH SPREAD II
POMAZÁNKY Z VAJEC

3 hard-cooked eggs
¼ pound bacon, cooked
    salt to taste

pepper to taste
chopped chives or sliced
    onion

Grind eggs and bacon together. Add salt and pepper. Decorate with chopped chives or sliced onion.

EGG SANDWICH SPREAD III
POMAZÁNKY Z VAJEC

3 hard-cooked eggs,
    chopped
7 tablespoons mayonnaise
    salt to taste

1 tablespoon Pickled
    Mushrooms, chopped
    (see Index)
1 tablespoon raw celery
    root, chopped

Blend together all ingredients.

RADISH AND CHEESE SPREAD

POMAZÁNKA Z ŘEDKVIČEK A SÝRA

½ cup butter
½ cup cream cheese
1 cup grated radishes

1 tablespoon chives
salt to taste

Cream butter, add remaining ingredients, and mix well. Serve with dark bread.

LIPTAUER CHEESE

LIPTOVSKÝ SÝR

½ pound farmer cheese
½ cup soft butter
¼ teaspoon mustard
1 tablespoon grated onion
1 tablespoon capers,
    chopped

1 sweet-sour pickle,
    chopped
¼ teaspoon paprika
salt to taste

Blend together all ingredients. Serve with dark bread.

CHEESE SPREAD WITH NUTS

SÝROVÁ POMAZÁNKA S OŘECHY

⅓ cup butter
⅓ cup ground walnuts
⅓ cup grated Swiss cheese

salt to taste
1 tablespoon milk (if
    needed)

Cream together butter, walnuts, and cheese. Add salt and mix well. Add milk if spread is too thick. Serve on rolls.

CONFECTIONS

NOUGAT
NUGÁT

¼ cup butter, softened
¼ cup sugar
1 egg, separated
1 tablespoon cocoa
¾ cup Dry Cake Crumbs
   (see Index)
2 tablespoons rum

1 tablespoon chopped
   candied orange peel
1 tablespoon chopped
   candied fruit
1 tablespoon chopped
   raisins
3 or 4 chopped apricot
   kernels

Cream butter with sugar. Blend in egg yolk, cocoa, half the cake crumbs, egg white, and rum. Mix the rest of the cake crumbs with chopped fruit (so pieces do not stick together). Blend both mixtures well. Shape into a roll about 1 inch thick. Wrap in parchment paper and put in a cool place to harden. Slice with a very sharp knife.

ALMOND PASTE (MARZIPAN)
MANDLOVÁ HMOTA

1 cup grated Blanched
   Almonds (see Index)
2 cups confectioners' sugar
1 egg white

icing (see Index)
cocoa (optional)
food colors (optional)

Mix together almonds and sugar. Add egg white. With a rolling pin, mash mixture to a smooth, pliable paste. Shape into small balls and dip into icing, or roll in cocoa. Or shape into tiny fruits or vegetables, let dry, then paint with food colors. Or roll out into a sheet and use to decorate cakes and pastries.

CHOCOLATE-COVERED FRUIT
OVOCE V ČOKOLÁDĚ

cubed fruit
Cocoa Icing (see Index)

Spear fruit pieces with toothpicks. Dip in icing. Stick tooth-picks into an inverted sieve so fruit can dry.

GLACÉED FRUIT
OVOCE V CUKRU

½ pound Crystal Sugar
   (see Explanatory
   Notes)
½ cup water

1 pound fruit (peaches,
   dates, tangerine sec-
   tions, orange sections,
   quartered apples, and
   quartered pears)

Sprinkle sugar with water and cook to hard-crack stage (see Sugar Stages and Temperatures). Remove from heat and place in a pan of hot water. Spear fruit pieces with toothpicks, dip in sugar. Make sure sugar does not touch toothpicks, or sugar coating may crack when toothpicks are removed.

CANDY FIGS
FÍKY

1 pound figs, ground
½ cup chopped candied
   citron
2 cups chopped walnuts

¼ cup sugar
1 egg, lightly beaten
½ cup Crystal Sugar (see
   Explanatory Notes)

Mix together all ingredients except Crystal Sugar, and shape into a roll about 1½ inches thick. Wrap in parchment paper and chill. Next day, slice about ½ inch thick, shape into figs, and roll in Crystal Sugar.

CAKE CRUMB BALLS

KULIČKY ZE SLADKÝCH DROBTŮ

½ cup plus 2 tablespoons
   butter
½ cup plus 2 tablespoons
   sugar

2⅓ cups Dry Cake Crumbs
   (see Index)
1 egg yolk
1 tablespoon rum

Cream butter with sugar until foamy. Add 1⅓ cups cake crumbs, egg yolk, and rum. Sprinkle a breadboard with remaining cake crumbs. Pinch off small pieces of the cake mixture and form into small balls; roll in crumbs. Serve in small fluted paper cups.

APPLE BALLS

JABLKOVÉ KULIČKY

¾ cup sugar
¼ cup water
1 pound sour apples,
   peeled, cored, and
   chopped
2 tablespoons chopped
   nuts

½ cup Crystal Sugar (see
   Explanatory Note) or
   Chocolate Icing (see
   Index)

Cook sugar and water to a thread (see Sugar Stages and Temperatures). Add apples, and cook about 20 minutes. Mix in nuts. Remove from heat and let cool slightly. Form into balls about 1 inch in diameter. Roll in Crystal Sugar, or cool and pour chocolate icing over them. Serves 4.

BLANCHED ALMONDS
SPAŘOVÁNÍ MANDLÍ

Plunge almonds into boiling water to cover. Bring to full boil. Cover, and let stand for 5 minutes. Drain. Slip off skins. Let almonds dry.

CHOCOLATE CHESTNUTS
KAŠTANY V ČOKOLÁDĚ

1 pound chestnuts,
  cooked and rubbed
  through a sieve
1¼ cups sugar

¾ cup water
1 teaspoon vanilla
Chocolate or Cocoa
  Icing (see Index)

Cook sugar and water to a thread (see Sugar Stages and Temperatures). Add chestnut purée (see Chestnut Cake for method) and vanilla, and continue to cook until thickened (about 10 minutes). Remove to a pastry board. Shape into small chestnuts. Spear each with a toothpick on the broad side. Dip in icing and stick through the holes in an inverted sieve to dry. Serves 4.

CANDY VERMICELLI
KAŠTANOVÁ MÍSA

3 tablespoons butter
½ cup sugar
1 pound chestnuts,
  cooked and rubbed
  through a sieve
1–2 tablespoons rum

⅓ cup ground nuts
1 cup Whipped Cream
  (see Index)
1 orange, sliced

Cream butter with sugar. Add chestnut purée (see Chestnut Cake for method), rum, and nuts. Force through a ricer held high above a platter. "Vermicelli" should be piled up lightly. Decorate with Whipped Cream and orange slices. Serves 4.

CANDIED ORANGE OR LEMON PEEL
KANDOVÁNÍ POMERANCŎVÉ A CITRÓNOVÉ KŮRY

orange or lemon peel   water
granulated sugar

Soak thick orange or lemon peel in water for 5 or 6 days, changing water daily. Drain. Cut into strips or desired small shapes. Weigh the peel and add to it equal amount of sugar. Add enough water to cover peel. Cook slowly until peel is transparent. Roll pieces in granulated sugar while still warm. Place on a baking sheet and let dry for about 24 hours on each side.

YOLK BONBONS
ŽLOUTKOVÉ BONBONY

3 tablespoons butter
½ cup plus 2 tablespoons
    sugar
2 hard-cooked egg yolks,
    mashed

1 teaspoon rum
    candied fruit pieces
1 tablespoon ground
    nuts
1–2 tablespoons Dry Cake
    Crumbs (see
    Index)

Cream butter and sugar thoroughly. Add egg yolks and rum. Make small balls of the mixture and press a piece of candied fruit into the center of each. Roll in ground nuts mixed with cake crumbs.

TOASTED FILBERTS
PRAŽENÍ LÍSKOVÝCH OŘÍŠKŮ

Toast filberts on a baking sheet in a preheated 350° oven until golden brown. Move and turn often. Rub in a cloth to remove skin.

GROG I
GROG

1 tablespoon sugar	boiling water
1 slice of lemon	rum to taste

Place sugar and lemon in a tall glass. Pour in water three-quarters full. Add rum and stir.

GROG II
GROG

1 cup water	¼ cup rum
¼ cup sugar	1 teaspoon butter
1 slice of lemon	

Cook water and sugar together for about 2 minutes. Add lemon and rum, and bring to a full boil. Remove from heat, add butter, stir. Pour into a glass and serve at once.

WINE GROG
GROG Z VÍNA

1 pint red wine	1 cinnamon stick
¾ cup sugar	4 slices of lemon

Bring wine, sugar, and cinnamon to a full boil. Strain into 2 glasses. Put 2 slices of lemon into each.

TURKISH COFFEE
TURECKÁ KÁVA

½ cup water	2 teaspoons very finely
1 teaspoon sugar	ground coffee

Heat water and sugar; add coffee. When coffee bubbles and rises, remove from heat. Let it settle, and bring to a boil again. Strain into cups.

Serves 2.

INDEX